Regiments at

Waterloo

RENÉ NORTH

ALMARK PUBLISHING CO. LTD., LONDON

First published—March 1971
Reprinted May 1971
Reprinted October 1971
Reprinted June 1972
Reprinted January 1974

ISBN 0 85524 024 5 (hard cover edition)
ISBN 0 85524 025 3 (paper covered edition)

Printed in Great Britain by
Martins Press Ltd., London EC1,
for the publishers, Almark Publishing Co. Ltd.,
49 Malden Way, New Malden,
Surrey KT3 6EA, England

Introduction

THIS new book on Waterloo can contribute little to the politi⌐ ⏉l and military history of the battle, especially in the limited compass of one ɪgle volume. Strategy, tactics, political causes and effects, all have been treated at length by eminent authorities, and no claim is made here to bring anything new to these particular aspects of a well-known story.

On the other hand, not much has been written about the participants in that highly significant struggle—the humble soldiers who just did as they were told, fighting in just another battle, and quite oblivious to the tremendous consequences of the outcome. Admittedly, many diaries and memoirs have survived from both sides, and have been ably edited; but what, in fact, did these men wear? What *should* they have worn? What was their background? How were they organized? So many questions needing so many answers.

This little book, therefore, is an attempt to supply some of those answers. An enormously exhaustive survey would necessarily border on the tedious, besides being an almost impossible task; nor could it be contained in one single handy volume. Thus, the erudite will detect some omissions, for which I apologize, with the explanation that I have tried here to keep to the more important points of interest even to beginners, and eliminate the others.

The intention, mainly, has been to give some idea of the dress, official or otherwise, of the troops involved—no easy task, because in many cases regulations were ignored while make-shift dress sometimes went unrecorded.

As many illustrations as possible have been included, and though the coloured figures do not show the backs, a careful examination of the drawings in the text will, by careful cross-reference, provide the information. Throughout this book the drawings in the text are numbered to key in with their respective captions. The colour drawings on pages 20, 21, 24, 25, 28, and 29 are also numbered and references to individual drawings on these pages are given in parentheses in the text, eg (Fig. 17). The old prints, both colour and half-tone, are from the author's personal collection except that on page 32 which is by courtesy of A. H. Bowling. For other pictures thanks are due to Mr. Lynn Sangster of Historex and the Regimental Museum of the Black Watch.

CONTENTS

3

HANOVERIAN ARMY

TRUMPETER LÜNEBURG HUSSARS

1815

ABOVE: The ornate elegance of military uniform at the time of the Battle of Waterloo is well shown in this painting, by the author, of a Lüneburg Hussars trumpeter. As in many other regiments the trumpeters' colours and facings were reversed. The jacket is red with blue facings but was blue with red facings for troopers, NCOs, and officers. See also page 35 and colour drawing Fig. 17. Note the trumpet slung across the back.

FRONT COVER: 1st Foot Guards (later the Grenadier Guards) at the time of Waterloo. See also page 17.

Part 1: The Anglo-Allied Army

'It all depends upon that article'
Wellington, pointing to a British soldier

OF about 97,000 men in the Allied armies at Waterloo, it may seem a little surprising that less than a third of that number were indigenous British troops, the rest being composed of Hanoverians, Dutch-Belgians, Brunswickers and Nassauers—to say nothing of the not inconsiderable contingent of The King's German Legion.

The Prussians, under Field-Marshal Blücher, have not been considered here, because the intention is to limit the subject to Wellington's command, which after all bore the brunt of the fighting. True, but for the timely arrival of the Prussians towards evening, the result might well have been different; but the fact remains that they were a separate entity and cannot be reckoned as an integral part of the Allied army. Nor should it be forgotten that when Blücher's 116,000 troops arrived, Napoleon found himself outnumbered by almost 2 to 1.

In the British army, new dress regulations had appeared in 1811, whose main effect was to introduce a totally new uniform for the Light Dragoons and an infantry shako with a high false front supposedly of 'belgic' derivation, which became known later as the 'Waterloo shako'. It had a short life, incidentally, because it 1816 it was replaced by one of bell-topped shape.

Non-commissioned officers' badges of rank, in the familiar chevron form, were worn on the right sleeve only (except in the Light Infantry), above the elbow. They were in white lace for sergeants and in regimental lace for corporals. The lance-corporal appeared at about this time, but his particular badge, if any, is not clear. (The name, derived from the French *l'ansepessade*, originated in turn from the Spanish *lanza pesada*. This denoted a cavalryman who had lost his mount in battle and therefore joined a foot unit, still carrying his lance. Being a horseman, he was superior to a mere foot-soldier, but inferior to a non-commissioned officer: hence the appointment, but not the rank, of lance-corporal.)

The British musket was the famous 'Brown Bess', whose chief difference from the French weapon was the absence of the two metal collars securing the barrel to the wooden stock.

The cavalry swords were of two patterns: straight for the heavy regiments and curved for the light.

Horse-furniture in the heavy cavalry consisted mostly of a sheepskin or blanket, with a scarlet cloak rolled and strapped over the pommel, and a scarlet valise at the back. In the light branch, a blue shabraque was used, with a round valise of the same colour, both items having a border in either yellow or white according to the buttons. (This can be taken as fairly general for all armies, since the colour of lace, loops, hat-ornaments, etc, are usually based on the same principle.)

British field officers wore two epaulettes and subalterns one only, on the right shoulder, while all had crimson sashes; and here again the metal of the epaulettes agreed with the buttons and loops.

HOUSEHOLD CAVALRY

The British Household troops, counterparts of the French Imperial Guard, consisted of no more than three regiments of cavalry and a like number of infantry, in marked contrast with the vast numbers of their opposite body.

The cavalry regiments were the 1st and 2nd Life Guards and the Royal Horse Guards. The first of these were descended from a corps of cavalier gentlemen raised by Charles II in 1660, and still take precedence over every other regiment in the army, unless the Royal Horse Artillery is present with its guns.

The 2nd Life Guards, also raised in 1660, were first styled 'The Duke of Albermarle's Troop of Guards'. In 1670 they became known as 'The Queen's Troop of Life Guards', but it was not until 1788 that the title of 2nd Life Guards was granted.

The Royal Horse Guards are more ancient still, since the regiment claims its origin from the Civil War, when it was a regiment of horse in the Parliamentarian forces. It was consequently to have been disbanded at the Restoration of 1660, but the King gave orders for its immediate re-establishment, and, contrary to the 2nd Life Guards, it has remained in existence ever since.

At Waterloo, the Life Guards wore red jackets with a dark blue collar-patch and turnbacks, and blue-grey overalls with a scarlet band. The lace and girdle were yellow, the latter bearing two crimson stripes, while the helmet had brass fittings, a black-over-crimson crest and a white plume. The 1st Life Guards wore yellow shoulder-straps and the 2nd blue, but for the rest the uniforms were identical.

The Royal Horse Guards were not officially recognized as Household Cavalry until 1820, but were nevertheless brigaded with the Life Guards. As

1   2

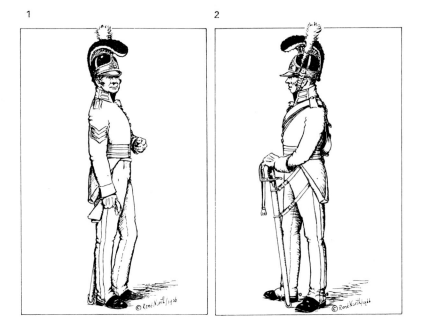

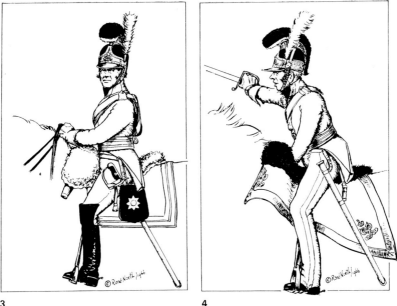

3   4

HOUSEHOLD CAVALRY

(1) Corporal of Horse, 1st Life Guards. All helmet-fittings, including the peak, were brass; and the frontal plate carried the interlaced Royal Cypher surmounted by a crown. The collar was red, with dark blue patches, each bearing two yellow loops. Cuffs and shoulder-straps were dark blue, the former edged in yellow; and the rank-stripes were gold.

(2) Trooper, Royal Horse Guards. The uniform is identical with the Life Guards' except that the jacket colours are reversed. The heavy cavalry sword was carried in a steel scabbard and a white sword-knot was attached to the hilt. It was a formidable weapon, intended for thrusting, with a wide blade.

(3) Trooper, The Life Guards. Note the short-slung sabretache. The star was brass.

(4) Officer, The Life Guards. Shabraques were dark blue in the Life Guards, and scarlet in the Royal Horse Guards.

such they assisted, with the rest of the Brigade, in repulsing the French counter-attack which developed after the charge of the Union Brigade. Their uniform, of the same pattern of the Life Guards, was dark blue with scarlet facings.

DRAGOON GUARDS

The title of Dragoon Guards originated in the early 18th century, when for reasons of economy several regiments of horse were converted to dragoons They were thus to receive less pay than hitherto, but as a rather meagre compensation were allowed the title of Guards, although never forming an integral part of the Household troops.

The 1st The King's Dragoon Guards, senior Horse Regiment of the Line (Fig 1), was brigaded with the Household Cavary and took part with the latter in the action in which they were attacked by Travers' 7th and 12th Cuirassiers

5   6

DRAGOONS

(5) Officer, The Royal Scots Greys. The cap-fittings are gold and the plume white. Jacket is scarlet with dark blue cuffs, collar and turnbacks, and gold lace. The sash is crimson, and the gloves and breeches white.

(6) Sergeant, The Royal Scots Greys. This is the service dress of the regiment, comprising blue-grey overalls with a dark blue band. Remainder as for officers, except yellow attributes where the officers' are gold. Note the gold sergeant's stripes on the right sleeve. At this period the regiment was also known as the North British Dragoons, and the initials NBD are carried on the saddle valise.

In the Ohain road, west of the cross-roads. The attack was repulsed, but the British, in their elation, galloped too far in pursuit and were thus compelled to retreat hurriedly in the face of a vigorous counter-attack by fresh regiments of Cuirassiers. Of the 2,000 men who charged originally, a bare 1,200 or 1,300 regained their original position behind La Haye Sainte.

This famous regiment, raised in 1685, was dressed in the uniform laid down for heavy cavalry, when a rather unserviceable hat was replaced by a black leather helmet somewhat resembling the French in design, with its brass comb and horsehair streamer. The frontal plate, also of brass, bore the interlaced Royal Cypher, and the regimental title appeared in a small oval underneath.

The jacket was ornamented with two rows of yellow lace running down the front from the top edge of the collar to the bottom of the jacket, which was fastened by hooks and eyes, thereby excluding the presence of any buttons. The facings, as befitted a Royal regiment, were dark blue.

DRAGOONS

If the King's Dragoon Guards were the only unit of that branch at Waterloo, the Dragoons were represented by three regiments: the 1st Royal Dragoons (Fig 2), the 2nd (Royal Scots Greys) and the 6th Inniskilling Dragoons— English, Scots and Irishmen forming the Union Brigade.

The 1st Dragoons was raised in 1661 for service in Tangier and originally wore cuirasses which were subsequently discarded. At Waterloo it was in the brigade which charged the French and galloped right into two divisional artillery batteries, and even reached Napoleon's Great Battery of 80 guns on its left. It was The Royals who attacked Bourgeois' 28th and 105th Regiments of the 1st Infantry Division.

The Royal Scots Greys were the only regular regiment of Scottish cavalry, and the only British cavalry regiment to wear the bearskin cap, granted in recognition of its capture of the Colours of the French *Régiment du Roi* at Ramillies in 1706.

Indeed, the feat was repeated at Waterloo in the memorable charge of the Union Brigade in which Sergeant Ewart took the Eagle of the 45th Line Regiment under Colonel Chapuzet, when the Greys, with Highlanders clinging to their stirrup-leathers, broke into Marcognet's 3rd Infantry Division with the exalted cry of 'Scotland for ever!'

The soldiers on the grey horses rightly earned the respect of their adversaries; and Napoleon's exclamation of *'Ces terribles chevaux gris'* was a fitting tribute to their bravery.

The third regiment of the Union Brigade, raised in 1689, became known as the '6th or Inniskilling Regiment of Dragoons' in the following year (Fig 3). At Waterloo, in the famous charge, its immediate objective was Donzelot's 2nd Infantry Division; but like its sister regiments, it penetrated too far into the enemy lines and came under a sharp counter-attack by the 3rd and 4th Chevaulégers-Lanciers. Fortunately, the 12th and 16th Light Dragoons were at hand and came to the rescue, thus enabling the survivors to regain their own lines in time.

This unit, not being a Royal regiment entitled to blue facings, wore yellow instead.

LIGHT DRAGOONS

Light Dragoons were formed in the British Army when, about the middle of the 18th century, the need for light cavalry made itself felt and several existing regiments were converted to that arm.

In 1812 the uniform underwent a radical change. The former crested helmet was replaced by a bell-topped shako of French inspiration, and the blue laced jacket gave place to one of plainer design, with collar, lapels, cuffs and turn-backs in the facing colour, so that the five regiments present at Waterloo appeared as follows:

Regiment	Facings and Girdle	Epaulettes	Buttons
11th	buff	white	silver
12th	yellow	white	silver
13th	buff	yellow	brass
16th	scarlet	white	silver
23rd	crimson	white	silver

The upper edge of the shako and the cap-lines were in the same colour as the epaulettes, and the girdle usually had two blue stripes lengthwise. White breeches and black hessian boots were worn on dress occasions, but in the field these were covered with blue-grey overalls normally bearing a double stripe in the facing colour. Shabraques were dark blue and, in most cases, carried ornaments in the facing colour.

For officers the dress was similar, except that their girdles were gold with

7   8

LIGHT DRAGOONS

(7) In full dress, officers wore white breeches and Hessian boots, but on active service these were replaced by blue-grey overalls, like the other ranks', with stripes in the facing colour (in this case, buff).

(8) Private, 12th Light Dragoons. This soldier is in dress uniform. The plumes are always white-over-red for all regiments.

two crimson stripes, and their cap-lines gold and crimson mixed. Epaulettes and suchlike attributes were gold or silver as the men's were yellow or white. The plume was white-over-red for all ranks, but whereas the officers carried sabretaches with gold or silver embroidery, the other ranks' pattern was plain black leather.

The 12th Light Dragoons was one of the regiments which came to the rescue of the Union Brigade, after their famous charge, by falling on the right flank of General Durutte's 4th Infantry Division (8th, 29th, 58th and 95th Line Regiments).

The regiment, raised in 1715, was one of those converted to Light Dragoons and served in India for an uninterrupted spell of 76 years. It also took part in the Peninsular War, and it is from that period that the custom arose for the band to play hymns every evening at tattoo, allegedly as a punishment for breaking into a nunnery. Another, more probable version, however, is simply that Pope Pius VI presented the music to the regiment with the request that it should be played by the band.

The 13th was stationed west of the Brussels road, alongside the 15th Hussars and the 2nd Light Dragoons of the King's German Legion. However, it was withdrawn just before the heavy attack on Hougoumont by Milhaud's IVth Cavalry Corps and Lefebvre-Desnoettes Light Cavalry of the Guard, consisting of eight Cuirassier regiments, with the Lancers, Chasseurs, Grenadiers and Dragoons of the Guard. It thus had the opportunity to harass the

9   10   11

LIGHT DRAGOONS

(9) Officer, 13th Light Dragoons. Taken from a print by Langendyk, this figure wears somewhat unconventional shako-ornaments; and the overall-stripe should be double, for light cavalry. Note also the gold 'waterfall' at the centre of the back, below the girdle.

(10) Cornet Polehill of the 16th Light Dragoons, wearing the old pattern laced jacket and barrelled sash of gilt and crimson. Curiously enough, the sabretache has gold ornaments, and not silver.

(11) 23rd Light Dragoons. Here, too, the laced jacket is in wear, and in this case the jacket is light blue. (From a contemporary print.)

Cuirassiers swirling around the British squares, but was compelled to fall back when attacked by the main body.

The 16th, posted on the left of the line, was brigaded with the 12th and therefore assisted in the relief of the Union Brigade after their rather unfortunate charge. In that action the 16th defeated a regiment of French lancers, rode straight through a battery of artillery and put as many as 40 guns out of action.

Later in the day, the two brigades of light cavalry being still intact and in perfect order, the 16th, with the 12th on its right, took part in the large-scale attack when six regiments rode down a square of the Imperial Guard, as well as a large number of Cuirassiers and artillery, taking 3,000 prisoners. It was in this action that some German dragoons mistook the 16th for French troops (the blue jackets may easily have looked green in the poor light) and the regiment narrowly escaped being attacked in the rear, thus giving substance to Wellington's objection to the new uniform as being, as he put it, 'too frenchified'.

In fact, the new dress was not issued to the 16th until 1814 and many officers wore the old laced jacket at Waterloo. Captain Luard, however, states in his memoirs that he wore regulation uniform during the battle, but that his lapels were white, which seems odd. On the other hand, a contemporary print shows Cornet Polehill of the 16th in the old laced jacket, but wearing regulation dress for the remainder.

The 23rd Light Dragoons which was present at Waterloo was one of two regiments bearing the same number almost at the same time: an extraordinary and confusing piece of duplication. The present regiment was disbanded in 1817, but is it interesting to recall that it was one of the four selected for conversion to Lancers after the French troops of that arm had wrought such havoc in the Union Brigade.

HUSSARS

The hussar branch of British light cavalry was not recognized officially until 1805, although the Prince Regent had already provided his own regiment, the 10th Light Dragoons, with many accoutrements of hussar pattern (Fig 5). Other regiments followed suit until authority finally had to concede the change, and eventually the 7th, 10th, 15th and 18th Light Dragoons were permitted rather grudgingly to call themselves Hussars and dress as such.

The Colonel of the 7th was the Marquess of Anglesey: the Lord Uxbridge of Waterloo fame. The 7th (Fig 4) had been very heavily engaged at Quatre Bras on June 16, and lost no fewer than 46 men on that day.

In the early stages of the battle of Waterloo the 10th Hussars were stationed on the left of the Allied line, on the right of the 11th, 12th and 16th Light Dragoons, when at about 12.30 a body of French troops advanced towards them. The 10th, however, was next moved to the centre, in support of the Brunswick Infantry, and towards the end of the battle, in company with the 18th and 1st Hussars of the King's German Legion, took part in Sir Hussey Vivian's final attacks on the enemy. These were probably the determining factor in the victory, for Sir Hussey, in a letter to a relative, says that the Commanding Officer of the 3rd Chasseurs of the Guard expressed the opinion that 'two regiments of British Hussars decided the affair'.

The 15th Hussars were descended from a regiment which acquired fame at the battle of Emsdorf, on June 16, 1760, when it defeated five battalions of French infantry and captured their Colours as well as nine guns. In recognition of that achievement the regiment was granted a lengthy battle honour stating the facts at length: a cumbersome feature later replaced by the device of crossed flags inverted, worn on the shabraque.

Another peculiarity of the regiment was the scarlet shako which was worn at Waterloo in lieu of the regulation busby (Fig 6). At the start of the battle, the regiment (brigaded with the 13th Light Dragoons) was stationed in first line at an angle in rear of Hougoumont Farm; but in the afternoon, after having withdrawn from that position, the 15th, together with the 13th, charged ten squadrons of French lancers. However, as it moved to the right it encountered a large body of Cuirassiers carrying all before them between Hougoumont and La Haye Sainte. The 15th and 13th immediately attacked, driving back the French cavalry and later took part in several other charges in the evening.

So far as the 18th Hussars are concerned (Fig 7), much private correspondence remains to inform us of their contribution to the fighting, from which one gathers that the regiment, with the 10th Hussars and the 1st Hussars of the King's German Legion, were in Sir Hussey Vivian's Brigade in position on the right of the lane leading to Verd Cocou, where they were used in support of the Nassauers and Brunswickers in the centre of the line. Later, the whole brigade was ordered forward towards La Belle Alliance, the 18th following the 10th, and the Germans in the rear. The 10th charged, and towards the evening the whole brigade encountered the French Imperial Guard: squares of infantry with Chasseurs à Cheval and Horse Grenadiers in the rear, though greatly diminished in numbers. In a further push forward, the 18th came up against troops of Cuirassiers and Lancers as well as infantry and guns, and were repulsed by a square on the top of a nearby knoll. However, the British cavalry soon regained the initiative and finally carried the day.

'I never saw such a day', wrote Sir Hussey Vivian. 'I expect . . . that every soldier will bear a medal with Mont St Jean on it'. ('Mont St Jean' was the first name proposed for the battle.)

ARTILLERY

Originating from 1793, the Royal Horse Artillery was formed to provide mobile artillery support for the cavalry, and therefore all personnel was mounted.

The crested helmet of 1815 was slightly larger than the original model, but the laced jacket was of distinct hussar inspiration, a curious convention which affected the dress of the Horse Artillery in a number of countries.

It was to this branch that Congreve's Rocket Troop was attached—an entirely new development in the field of firearms. Rocket gunners carried a bundle of rocket-sticks in a small bucket forward of the offside stirrup and four 6-pounder rockets in two specially constructed holsters. An effective drill was devised, and the weapon, though perhaps not as deadly as expected, had considerable demoralizing value. It was, of course, the forerunner of the huge long-range rockets of today.

The Foot Artillery was much older than the Horse, having been founded on May 26, 1716, in replacement of the 'trains of artillery' which used to be raised at the start of a campaign and disbanded at its close. It became a Royal regiment in 1722 and has remained so to this day.

The uniform, except in its early years, was always blue, with red facings, so

12

Serjeant, 1814

ROYAL HORSE ARTILLERY

HELMET: White plume. Blue turban. Brass fittings.
JACKET. Blue. Scarlet collar and cuffs. Yellow lacing and chevrons. Brass buttons. Crimson sash.
OVERALLS: Grey. Scarlet stripes.
BELT, GLOVES, SLINGS: White.
SWORD: All-steel. White knot.

(after Denis Dighton, in Reynolds MSS)

13

ROYAL HORSE ARTILLERY
Driver and Gunner

HELMETS: White plume. Blue turban. Brass fittings.
JACKETS: Blue. Scarlet collar, cuffs, shoulder-straps, turnbacks. Yellow lacing. Brass buttons.
OVERALLS: Grey. Scarlet stripes. White buttons.
SWORD: All-steel. White knot.

(after Macdonald "Hist. Dress R.A." and Reynolds MSS)

15

ROYAL REGT. OF ARTILLERY
Field Officer, 1815
SHAKO: White plume. Gilt plate. Gold cords.
JACKET: Blue. Scarlet collar, lapels, cuffs, turnbacks.
  Gold loops and buttons.
SASH: Crimson.
BREECHES, GLOVES: White.
SWORD: Gilt fittings. Gold knot.

ROYAL REGT. OF ARTILLERY
Gunner, 1814
SHAKO: White ornaments. Brass plate.
JACKET: Blue. Scarlet collar, shoulder-straps, cuffs,
  turnbacks. Yellow lace. Brass buttons.
BELTS, BREECHES, POUCH: White. Brass plate.
  (after Hamilton Smith, "Cost. of Army")

that by the time of Waterloo a gunner looked like an infantryman in reversed colours: 'belgic' cap, laced jacket and blue-grey trousers, or white breeches and black gaiters for home duty.

    The artillery drivers belonged to a separate corps and wore a uniform combining the yellow-laced, square-cuffed jacket of the Foot Artillery with the helmet and overalls of the Horse branch.

    The total number of Royal Artillery troops engaged at Waterloo amounted to 48 guns and 1,400 men in the Horse Artillery, and 54 guns and 3,630 men in the Foot.

FOOT GUARDS

    The original Foot Guards of the Restoration were raised partly for ceremonial duties in London, partly for active service abroad; and it is interesting to observe that from the very start they were dressed in red coats.

    These, then, were the 1st Foot Guards (now the Grenadier Guards). The 2nd Regiment was originally a unit of the Parliamentary army; but in January 1660, from its station at Coldstream, it marched to London as Monk's Regiment of Foot to assist in the Restoration of Charles II on his return to England from the Netherlands. The regiment, henceforth based on the capital, not unnaturally became known to the inhabitants as 'the soldiers from Coldstream' and has never relinquished that title, though in a different form.

    The 3rd Foot Guards were descended from a regiment reputedly raised as long ago as 1642. Its early history, however, is obscure; but it was not until 1877 that Queen Victoria restored its original title of The Scots Guards.

    By 1815 the three regiments were brigaded together as The Guards Brigade and wore the regulation red infantry jacket of the British Army. The facings, on collar, cuffs and shoulder-straps, were of the dark blue reserved for Royal

16   **17**

FOOT GUARDS

(16) This officer of the 1st Foot Guards is wearing full dress: an all-scarlet coat with gold lace and epaulettes, white breeches, gaiters, belt and gloves, and a crimson sash. The plume is white and the cap-plate gilt. This is the dress of the grenadier company.

(17) Sergeant, 2nd Foot Guards. The jacket is scarlet, as for officers; and the plume white-over-red, denoting a battalion company. For grenadiers it would be white, and for the light company green. Note the pike (replacing the 18th century spontoon) which was the normal weapon for sergeants.

regiments, and the breeches were white, worn with black under-knee gaiters. On active service, however, these were exchanged for blue-grey trousers.

The shako, of regulation 'belgic' pattern, was often enclosed in an oilskin cover, but on dress occasions it was ornamented with white cords for the grenadier and battalion companies, and green for the light infantry. On ceremonial duties, the grenadiers wore a bearskin cap with a brass plate in front. Plumes were white for grenadiers, white-over-red in the battalions, and green for the light companies.

The flank companies (ie, grenadiers and light infantry) were further distinguished by wings worn at the tip of the shoulders, whereas the battalion companies simply had a tuft of white worsted. It was on the jacket, too, that the regimental distinctions appeared, since the 1st Foot Guards wore their buttons—and the attendant loops—equally spaced, while in the 2nd they were in pairs, and in threes in the 3rd. These loops were of 'bastion' shape (ie, ending in a point shaped like a pike or an arrow-head) in the 1st Guards, but ending in a plain point in the other two regiments.

The Guards Brigade's main action at Waterloo was its stubborn defence of Hougoumont Farm on the right of the Allied line. The buildings, situated as they were in the low ground between the two armies, formed a major strong-point whose possession became a vital asset on the terrain. The Guards held on

FOOT GUARDS

(18) Private, 1st Foot Guards. The equipment would normally include a blue water-bottle and white haversack on the left hip. Compare with colour plate opposite which shows the same uniform from the back and serves as a colour guide to this drawing.

18

grimly throughout the battle, in spite of repeated and heroic attempts by French infantry to break down the gate. Indeed, we shall see further that an officer of the 1st Light Infantry actually effected a breach, but was killed in the process.

PRIVATES *of the* FIRST REGIMENT *of* FOOT GUARDS.
on SERVICE.

ABOVE: Colour view of men of the 1st Foot Guards at the time of the Battle of Waterloo, and showing both front and rear detail. Compare with drawing 18 and also Infantry of the Line drawings 19 to 23 whose uniform was in the same colours. Note that the trousers could be worn inside or outside the gaiters. LEFT: A private of the 13th Light Dragoons in the blue-grey overalls and dark blue jacket as described on page 9. Both these near-contemporary prints come from Charles Hamilton Smith's famous book 'Costume of the Army of the British Empire according to the Last Regulations, 1814'. (Author's collection).

19   20   21

INFANTRY OF THE LINE

The British infantry regiments, unlike the French, were each distinguished by special characteristics of dress. Every one had its particular facing colour and lace, as well as its own arrangement of buttonhole loops (either in singles or in pairs) which could be in three shapes: pointed, square-ended or bastion In addition, officers' epaulettes and lace could be either gold or silver. Thus every regiment looked different from its neighbour; and where, in spite of this, duplication still existed, the colour of the lines in the lace would mark the difference. Bandsmen frequently wore reversed colours (Fig 15).

Thus, the dress of the British Line regiments engaged at Waterloo can be summed up as follows:

Regiment	Facings	Loops	Officers' Lace
1st	blue	pairs, square	gold
4th	blue	singles, bastion	silver
14th	buff	pairs, square	silver
23rd	blue	singles, bastion	gold
25th	blue	singles, bastion	gold
27th	buff	singles, square	gold
28th	yellow	pairs, square	silver
30th	light yellow	singles, bastion	silver
32nd	white	pairs, square	gold
37th	yellow	pairs, square	silver
40th	buff	pairs, square	gold
44th	yellow	singles, square	silver
54th	green	pairs, square	silver
59th	white	singles, bastion	gold
69th	green	pairs, square	gold
73rd	dark green	singles, bastion	gold
78th	buff	singles, bastion	gold
81st	buff	pairs, pointed	silver
84th	yellow	pairs, square	silver
91st	yellow	pairs, square	silver

An interesting feature is the fact that the 91st, although Highlanders, did

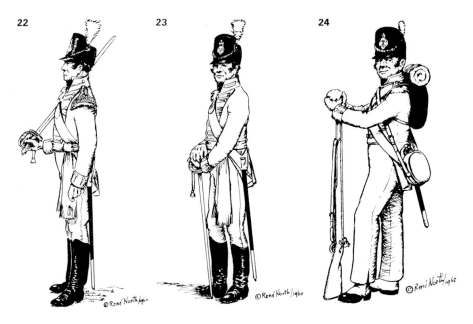

INFANTRY OF THE LINE

(19) Drummers frequently wore reversed colours; in this case—the 54th Foot—a bright green jacket with red facings. The drum, too, is green, with red and white diagonals on the hoops. The central design is a blue circle enclosed in a red ring. All lace is white, and the trousers and gaiters are the regulation blue-grey.

(20) Grenadier, 44th Foot. Flank companies were distinguished by red wings at the shoulders. These were trimmed in regimental lace and carried a short white fringe at the edge. The plume and cords were white for grenadiers and green for the light companies. This figure is wearing the white breeches prescribed for home duty.

(21) Private, 54th Foot. Most units wore an oilskin cover over their shakos on the day of the battle because of the heavy thunderstorms that prevailed. Packs were not subject to regulations, and regiments generally made their own arrangements, in most cases painting the numeral on the outer flap.

(22) Grenadier Officer, 28th Foot. Note the wings (silver in this regiment) of the Grenadier Company. The grenadier officer's sword is really slightly curved, though this is not readily apparent in this view.

(23) Officer, 1st Foot. This is the senior line regiment of the British Army: the Royal Scots. A single epaulette on the right shoulder denotes an officer of the battalion companies, and the dark blue facings a Royal regiment.

(24) Private, 4th Foot. This soldier belongs to a battalion company, and his plume, therefore, is white-over-red. The worsted shoulder-tufts are white.

not wear the kilt. This was restored to them in 1821 and they eventually became the 1st Battalion of the Argyll and Sutherland Highlanders. They were one of the regiments detailed to watch over Napoleon at St Helena, and the Emperor was very complimentary to all ranks.

A detailed account of the various actions of the Line regiments is impossible in this short exposition; but their place in the order of battle will be found elsewhere in this book, and the serious student is referred to the numerous regimental histories which are readily available.

ANGLO-ALLIED REGIMENTS

(1) 1st Dragoon Guards, Private. (2) 1st Royal Dragoons, Private. (3) 6th Inniskilling Dragoons, Officer. (4) 7th Hussars, Private. (5) 10th Hussars, Private. (6) 15th Hussars, Private. (7) 18th Hussars, Private. (8) 1st Hussars, The King's German Legion, Officer. (9) 2nd Hussars, K.G.L., Officer. (10) 3rd Hussars, K.G.L., Private.

ANGLO-ALLIED REGIMENTS

(11) Royal Staff Corps, Private. (12) Royal Engineers. (13) Royal Sappers and Miners, Sapper. (14) Royal Waggon Train, Private. (15) 30th Foot, Fifer (16) Bremen and Verden Hussars, Private. (17) Lüneburg Hussars, Trumpeter. (18) Cumberland Hussars, Private. (19) K.G.L. Line regiment, Sergeant-Major. (20) K.G.L. Light regiment, Private.

HIGHLANDERS

(25) Colour-Sergeant, 42nd Foot. The scarlet jacket has a blue collar, shoulder-straps and cuffs; and the kilt is of the sombre 'Government' tartan peculiar to the Black Watch. The sash, knotted on the right, is crimson, and the hose are white with pink stripes. The colour-sergeant's rank-badge, on the right sleeve only, consists of a Union Flag and crossed swords in full colour beneath a crown and above a single white chevron. The bonnet has a red, white and black dice-border and a red hackle.

(26) Officer, 79th Foot. The facings here—on collar, lapels and cuffs—are of a dark but bright green, and the lace, epaulettes and buttons are gold. The plume is white-over-red, and the hose as in the 42nd. The tartan of the 79th is a colourful sett predominantly dark blue, but with a generous proportion of red and a distinctive yellow line. Buttons were in distinct pairs, not apparent here where they are partly obscured by cross-belts.

(27) Corporal, Grenadier Company, 92nd Foot. Whereas officers' and sergeants' jackets were scarlet, those of the other ranks were red. The wings and white hackle proclaim the grenadier, but for the rest the uniform is the regulation other ranks' pattern. The facings are yellow and the kilt much resembles that of the 42nd except that here a yellow line is present in the pattern, forming large squares.

HIGHLANDERS

Three regiments of kilted Highlanders took part in the battle: the 42nd (The Black Watch), the 79th (The Queen's Own Cameron Highlanders) and the 92nd (2nd Battalion The Gordon Highlanders).

The 42nd and 92nd were brigaded together in the 9th Brigade, under Sir Denis Pack, with the 1st Foot (The Royal Scots) and the 2nd Battalion of the 44th. The 79th was the only Scottish regiment in Sir John Kempt's 8th Brigade. All these splendid regiments, which had seen heavy fighting at Quatre Bras, were now posted on the left centre of the Allied line, where they were drawn up, in greatly diminished numbers, just north of the Ohain road—that fateful sunken road where so much fighting occurred, to the east of La Haye Sainte.

The French infantry advanced as far as the hedge bordering this road and then halted to gather strength for their final charge, when the 92nd were ordered to attack with the bayonet. Picton then sent his whole division forward, and as he led the charge he was shot dead. It was at that moment that the Union Brigade came through to carry out their impetuous attack, and some of the Highlanders, in a somewhat undisciplined burst of enthusiasm, grasped the Greys' stirrup-leathers and charged with them.

The Black Watch (42nd), the oldest of the Highland regiments, was descended from the independent companies of Scottish gentlemen raised in the early 17th century to keep order in the Highlands. Their name, often explained as reflecting the dark colour of their tartan, really derives from the original duty of the Watch. namely to prevent marauding bands of Highlanders from collecting 'black meal' from the inhabitants. This was a highly illegal levy, demanded with menaces, and the word has now passed into current speech as 'blackmail'.

The 79th was raised by Cameron of Erracht in 1793, and was thus only 22 years old when it fought at Waterloo—the same age, incidentally, as the Royal Horse Artillery. After being in action at Quatre Bras on June 16, the regiment bivouacked on the night of the 17th in the rain-sodden fields near La Haye Sainte. Next morning, the French began the attack at about 10.30, with their infantry bearing down on the 79th and 28th. They were successfully repulsed, but Napoleon now brought up his cavalry. The 79th formed square, and then, to their surprise and admiration, Piper Kenneth Mackay stepped out of the ranks to cheer his comrades with the strains of 'Cogadh na Sith'.

The 79th suffered heavily in the battle, for out of the 43 officers and 735 other ranks that set out from Brussels three days earlier, only 9 officers and 288 men remained to bivouac at La Belle Alliance that night.

'Black Watch of the battles; first to come and last to go'. The 42nd lived up to its watchword, for Waterloo was only one of the many battles in which the red hackle was worn with pride and distinction. This scene shows the fighting near Quatre Bras. (Courtesy Black Watch Regimental Museum).

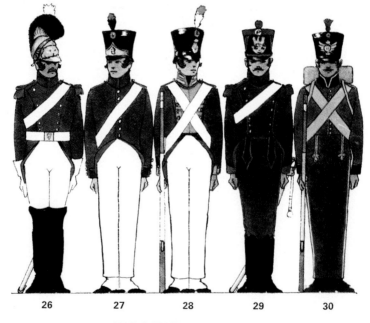

ANGLO-ALLIED AND FRENCH

(21) Brunswick Advance Guard, Rifleman. (22) Brunswick Hussars, Private. (23) Brunswick Lancers, Private. (24) Brunswick Artillery, Gunner. (25) 1st Brunswick Infantry, Private. (26) Belgian Carabiniers, Private. (27) Dutch-Belgian Artillery, Gunner. (28) Dutch Indian Infantry, Private. (29) French Horse Artillery, Gunner. (30) Nassau Infantry, Private.

FRENCH REGIMENTS

(31) Chasseurs of the Guard, Private. (32) Chasseurs of the Guard, Officer. (33) Horse Grenadiers of the Guard, Private. (34) Horse Grenadiers of the Guard, Private (field service order). (35) Dragoons of the Guard, Private. (36) Lancers of the Guard, Private. (37) Sapper of the Guard. (38) 6th Chasseurs, Private. (39) 1st Chasseurs, Elite company. (40) 3rd Lancers, Private.

LIGHT INFANTRY

(28) Private, 51st Foot. All light infantry regiments wore wings at the shoulders and a green plume in the cap, which was usually fitted with a brass bugle-horn in front as a badge.

(29) 52nd Foot. The private is carrying the light infantry musket which was introduced about this time, but probably not used at Waterloo; while the officer wears silver wings and the curved light infantry sword.

LIGHT INFANTRY

As a fairly recent development in the British Army, the light infantry was first organized by Sir John Moore during his service in Minorca (1803) on the pattern of the French *voltigeurs*, after he had observed Major Mackenzie's system of breaking up a battalion into skirmishers, supports and reserves. He therefore introduced the system in his own regiment, the 52nd.

The uniform of these troops was almost identical with that of the light companies of the Line battalions, except that the shako was replaced by a black felt 'conical' cap.

Three light infantry regiments were present at Waterloo: the 51st (later The King's Own Yorkshire Light Infantry), the 52nd (later the 2nd Battalion The Oxfordshire and Buckinghamshire Light Infantry) and the 71st (The Highland Light Infantry). Their jackets were of regulation infantry pattern, with blue facings for the 51st and buff for the other two. The loops were pointed and in pairs for the 51st, square in pairs for the 52nd, and square in singles for the 71st; and the officers wore gold lace in the 51st and silver in the others. However, the 71st wore dark blue caps in the rank and file, with the diced border peculiar to Scottish regiments.

The 51st was in the 4th Brigade, with the 14th and 23rd Foot, on the extreme right of the Allied line, west of the Nivelle road, and therefore was not heavily engaged. After the battle, however, they entered Hougoumont Farm, where Wheeler, the diarist, records, 'I had the honour of cooking a beefsteak in the steel jacket belonging to one of the Cuirassiers'.

The 52nd, also in position near Hougoumont, did not come into action until

LIGHT INFANTRY

(30) 71st Highland Light Infantry. Sergeants of light infantry wore their sashes cross-wise and carried a whistle on the cross-belt. Their chevrons appeared on both sleeves and instead of a pike, as in the Line, they were armed with a short musket. The bugler wears reversed colours.

30

the close of the battle, when they were attacked by the 3rd Foot Chasseurs in that last and vital action of the Imperial Guard. However, with the 71st they formed square and eventually joined in the final advance after the commanding officer, Sir Colin Colbourne, had initiated the brilliant flanking movement which, according to some, ensured the victory.

THE RIFLE BRIGADE

(31) The green uniform of these troops was so dark that it appeared almost black; but the most curious feature is the unaccountable fashion for officers of this corps to copy the hussar dress. The Baker rifle shown here was much shorter than the 'Brown Bess' and the grooved bore of the barrel imparted a spin to the bullet, as in present-day weapons. The rifle would not accommodate a bayonet, so riflemen, then as now, 'fixed swords'.

31

THE RIFLE BRIGADE

The only British rifle regiment at Waterloo was the 95th (The Rifle Brigade) whose sombre green and black uniform formed a marked contrast with the

FRENCH REGIMENTS

(41) 1st Hussars, Private. (42) 4th Hussars, Private. (43) 5th Hussars, Private. (44) 6th Hussars, Private. (45) 7th Hussars Private. (46) Tirailleur of the Guard. (47) Voltigeur of the Guard. (48) Sailor of the Guard, Private. (49) Sailor of the Guard (field service order). (50) Foot Chasseur of the Guard (field service order).

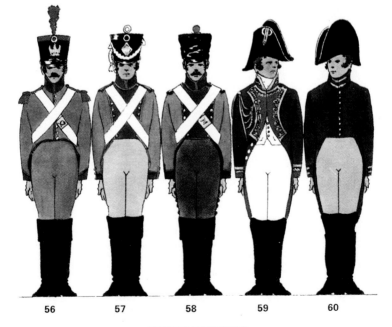

FRENCH REGIMENTS

(51) 5th Lancers, Trumpeter in Imperial livery. (52) A.D.C. to divisional commander. (53) Infantry of the Line, Officer. (54) Infantry of the Line, Voltigeur (field service order). (55) 2nd Swiss Regiment, Private. (56) Artillery Driver of the Guard. (57) Artillery Driver. (58) Transport Driver. (59) Senior Surgeon. (60) Veterinary Surgeon, Heavy Cavalry.

red coats of the Line.

This was the corps that was raised at the turn of the century and numbered 95th in August 1800. It was modelled on the 60th (The King's Royal Rifle Corps), a body descended from the 5th Battalion of The Royal American Regiment: a special battalion of light troops designed to counteract the activities of the American Rangers in the War of Independence. It was dressed in dark green, after the style of the German Jaegers, and its drill and tactics were devised on lines hitherto unheard of, for the soldier was taught to think for himself, to be self-reliant and to act on his own initiative, rather than to move in the dense formations of the Line.

The Rifles had been hardly pressed at Quatre Bras, and again at Waterloo, when two companies found themselves in the thick of the fighting in a gravel pit near La Haye Sainte. So fierce were the French attacks that the riflemen were unable to maintain contact with the defenders inside the buildings and were forced to withdraw. At about 3 o'clock, however, they regained possession of a mound near the farm, but were later driven off when the French captured the position. Yet they soon reformed and put up a stout defence against the repeated charges of the Cuirassiers.

STAFF CORPS, ENGINEERS AND TRANSPORT

The Cavalry Staff Corps was raised in April 1813 to act as a form of military police and to undertake the orderly duties previously performed by cavalrymen detached from their units.

The Corps was dressed in a light dragoon uniform, but here the jacket was scarlet with blue facings, and the overalls had a double blue stripe (Fig 11). The horse-furniture consisted of a small saddle-cloth with a narrow white border, surmounted by a circular red valise bearing the initials 'S.D.' on the ends, above the letter of the particular troop. A grey cloak was rolled and strapped over the pommel of the saddle.

The Staff Corps was disbanded in 1814, but hurriedly re-raised in the following year after Napoleon's sudden return from Elba.

There was also a dismounted branch of the Corps, but it is not clear whether it served in the present campaign. The uniform was of infantry pattern, with a grenadier's white plume on the shako, but the red jacket was a plain single-breasted garment without any loops. Cuffs, collar and shoulder-straps were dark blue, the last two items edged in white lace. A white cross-belt ran over the left shoulder and the dress was completed by a white waist-belt with a brass plate. The breeches were dark blue, encased in black mid-calf gaiters.

In the early days of military engineering, the appropriate organization consisted entirely of officers. They were later assisted by a separate body of military artificers which subsequently became the Royal Corps of Sappers and Miners (Fig 13). The officers, however, remained a different entity, entitled The Royal Engineers and originally dressed in blue. Early in the Napoleonic Wars, however, this often caused them to be mistaken for French officers and in consequence the uniform was changed to scarlet (Fig 12).

Another vital service, the transport, was represented at Waterloo by units of the Royal Waggon Train. Few bodies of the British Army have so many times changed their title and dress: Corps of Waggoners; Royal Waggon Train; Land Transport; Commissariat Corps; Army Service Corps, and finally the present-day Royal Corps of Transport being among the titles.

The Royal Waggon Train dated from 1799, and was clothed in a blue uniform and raised for service in the North Holland Expedition under the command of a Waggon Master General with the rank of lieutenant-colonel. It was formed from men drafted from various cavalry regiments, the junior officers being mostly former troop quartermasters and sergeants. In 1811 the colour of the jacket was altered to red (Fig 14) and by 1814 there were 14 troops in existence, with a total of 1,903 other ranks; but despite its fine record of service the Corps was disbanded at Hythe in March 1833 after having served in the two Peninsular Wars as well as at Waterloo.

THE KING'S GERMAN LEGION: LIGHT DRAGOONS

During the Continental wars of 1801–6, the Kingdom of Hanover, closely associated as it was with the British Crown, found itself in an extremely uneasy position, being occupied alternately by France and Prussia. Small wonder, then, that attempts were made to regain contact with Great Britain by encouraging a more or less clandestine enlistment of recruits for the British service.

Thus, on August 10, 1803, King George III charged Baron Decken with the raising of a corps of light infantry to be called The King's Germans. By November, 450 recruits had arrived in the Isle of Wight, and, as prospects seemed encouraging, it was resolved to extend the establishment to cavalry and artillery as well, and to name the entire force The King's German Legion.

The first cavalry units were equipped as heavy dragoons, but these were later converted to two regiments of light dragoons and dressed much as their

THE KING'S GERMAN LEGION: LIGHT DRAGOONS

(32) Officers, 1st Light Dragoons. The left-hand figure is in the white breeches worn in full dress, while the other wears the overalls for field service. Note the unconventional shape of the sabretaches.

(33) Officer, 2nd Light Dragoons. The falling plume may be peculiar to this regiment. In full dress a dark blue sabretache was in use, with crowned Royal Cypher, scroll and border in silver embroidery, as shown in the detail close-up.

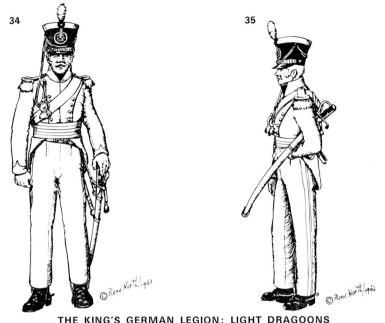

THE KING'S GERMAN LEGION: LIGHT DRAGOONS

(34 and 35) Privates, 1st and 2nd Light Dragoons. The style of dress is identical with the British light dragoons. Even the sword is the same and the only difference is in the colourings.

British counterparts. The uniform was substantially the same in both regiments' the only difference being gold/yellow ornaments for the 1st, and silver/white ones for the 2nd.

At Waterloo, both these regiments, brigaded together with the British 23rd Light Dragoons in Sir W. Dörnberg's 3rd Brigade, took little part in the early stages of the battle, but the 1st Regiment, after having been in second line behind the 3rd Division until about 2 p.m., was ordered at about 4 o'clock to assist the 23rd in repulsing the Cuirassiers harassing the British squares.

The 2nd Light Dragoons, also on the same mission. eventually joined the other two regiments in the final advance after 6 o'clock.

THE KING'S GERMAN LEGION: HUSSARS AND ARTILLERY

The three hussar regiments of The King's German Legion were distinguished chiefly by their headdress: a black busby for the 1st (Fig 8), a brown one for the 2nd and a black shako for the 3rd (Fig 10). The pattern shown here (Fig 9) is a little unusual with its black leather peak, and appears to be peculiar to the K.G.L., since it was also worn by the rank-and-file in the 1st and in black fur by the officers of the 3rd.

The latter regiment, brigaded with the 3rd Light Dragoons in Colonel Arentschild's 7th Cavalry Brigade, was first stationed near La Haye Sainte in front of Ompteda's Brigade, but was forced to retire. South of Hougoumont,

LEFT : Guardroom, Grenadiers of the Imperial Guard. This contemporary French print showing various dress styles, appear mostly full dress. Note the undress cap worn by some men. The drummer on the extreme right should have gold lacing around his cuffs. (A. H. Bowling collection).

however, it later charged and broke a body of Cuirassiers, but was beaten back with heavy losses.

The 1st Hussars were with the 10th and 18th (British) Hussars in Sir Hussey Vivian's 6th Brigade, and the 2nd Hussars were with the 7th and 15th in Sir Colquhoun Grant's 5th Brigade.

The Horse and Foot Artillery uniforms were exact replicas of the British model, the only difference appearing in the Horse Artillery, where the red cuffs were cut square, and not pointed. These were edged along the top in yellow lace, which also described a wide round loop where one would normally expect a crow's foot or an Austrian knot. Another distinction was the white leather crossbelt, slung over the right shoulder, and bearing a brass buckle in the centre.

THE KING'S GERMAN LEGION: INFANTRY OF THE LINE

The infantry of the Legion, like the Light Dragoons and Hussars, was clothed in a uniform so closely resembling the British as to make identification almost impossible (Fig 19). But before examining the subject more closely, the following extract from N. Ludlow Beamish's *History of the King's German Legion* will prove interesting.

It is dated December 1803 and states: 'The original plan of forming one regiment only was now extended, and a corps consisting of cavalry, infantry and artillery was proposed to be raised. The better to effect this object, the independent levies of Colonel von der Decken and Major Halkett were ordered to be discontinued, and the men that had already been enlisted by those officers to be incorporated as the basis of a legion, which his majesty was pleased to authorize should be raised by his royal highness the Duke of Cambridge'.

THE KING'S GERMAN LEGION: LIGHT INFANTRY

There were two light infantry battalions in The King's German Legion, both dressed similarly to the British Rifle Brigade, except that in this case a pair of black wings was worn at the tip of the shoulders (Fig 20). The buttons were silver, and the only difference between the two units was the setting of these on the jacket, for in the 1st Battalion they appeared in one row of 12, in the 2nd there was one additional row on each side of the garment, running from the shoulders to the waist.

The officers of the 1st Battalion wore the same conical cap as the men, but their wings were the all-silver variety common to British light infantry officers. In the 2nd Battalion, however, the pattern was somewhat different. The head-dress was a black 'Flügelmütze' or mirliton: that peculiar article much favoured by the early hussars and resembling, in this case, a regulation conical cap without a peak.

The jacket, in a very dark green, was ornamented with black hussar braiding, and the wings here were replaced by the same black cording retained by a silver button near the collar.

Officers wore white gloves, and their sash was of the wide crimson variety, worn around the waist and terminating in crimson cords and tassels after the manner of the British light infantry.

The K.G.L. light infantry battalions were in Colonel von Ompteda's 2nd Brigade (1st and 2nd Light Battalions, and 5th and 8th Line Battalions) in Sir Charles Alten's 3rd Division, while the remainder of the line battalions formed the 1st K.G.L. Brigade under Colonel du Plat (1st, 2nd, 3rd and 4th) in Sir H. Clinton's 2nd Division.

HANOVERIAN HUSSARS

Three hussar regiments were raised in 1813: Lüneburg, Bremen-and-Verden and The Duke of Cumberland's Volunteer Hussars.

In the Bremen-and-Verden Regiment (Fig 16) the 1st and 4th Squadrons wore a bell-topped shako of British design, but the 2nd and 3rd had a brown fur busby with a tall white plume in front and cap-lines in the Guelphic colours of yellow and white. The busby-bag, hanging on the right, was red. For horse-furniture, this regiment had a green shabraque, to correspond with the green of the jacket, with a broad red border. There were no ornaments, and the round valise was green likewise, with a narrow red border at the ends.

The Lüneburg Hussars wore a blue jacket with a red collar and cuffs, and a red pelisse with white fur. The busby was similar to Bremen-and-Verden's except that the plume was red and the bag blue. Trumpeters wore reversed colours and white busbies with a red bag (Fig 17). The shabraque, ending in a sharp point as in the 1st Regiment, was blue and edged in red triangular vandykes, probably edged in white. Here again, no ornaments appeared on the shabraque.

The officers' uniform was basically the same as for the other ranks, except that the lacing was silver instead of white; but in what was known as 'gala' dress they wore red breeches with silver bands and Austrian knots, and a bicorne hat with a white plume.

The Cumberland Hussars (Fig 18), a unit of raw and inexperienced troops under an incompetent commanding officer, proved to be more of a liability than an asset. So long as they were held in reserve they were steady enough, but close action was not their *forte*. When the 3rd Hussars of the K.G.L were driven back behind the squares after their charge near Hougoumont, Lord Uxbridge ordered the Cumberland Hussars to counter-attack; but their cautious approach to the enemy was so hesitant that the exalted Frenchmen, already elated by their previous success, not only stopped them, but sent them flying back in panic. According to Fortescue, they did not stop until they reached Brussels, with the alarming news that the battle was lost. Schwertfeger, on the other hand, informs us with delightful *naïveté* that the commanding officer withdrew the regiment, 'but forgot to bring it back again'.

HANOVERIAN INFANTRY AND ARTILLERY

Like their compatriots of The King's German Legion, the Hanoverian infantrymen were dressed in uniforms closely imitated from the British: red jackets and blue-grey trousers for the Line regiments and a very dark green for the rifle units, which were called light battalions. None of these appears to have been numbered, but they were known by such names as Bremen, Lüneburg, Grubenhagen, etc.

We find them mostly in the 1st Division under Lt-Gen. Sir Charles Alten, where six of these battalions formed Major-Gen. Count Kielmansegge's 1st Hanoverian Brigade, while in the 4th Division under Sir Colin Colville, five battalions made up Major-Gen. Sir Charles Lyon's 6th Hanoverian Brigade.

It was in the 4th Division, too, that the Hanoverian artillery served: Rettberg's and Braun's field batteries working alongside Brome's Royal Artillery troops and numbering a total of 12 guns. The gunners' uniform was probably based upon the British pattern, as in the K.G.L., although there is no concrete evidence to that effect.

To return to the infantry, it is interesting to note that several *Landwehr* units were employed. These were second-line troops—a kind of militia—and were to

HANOVERIAN INFANTRY AND ARTILLERY

(36) Officer, Bremen Regiment. The position of the plume, in the front of the 'belgic cap, is odd, and may be a faulty recording by an eye-witness. The wings and cross-belt, also, seem out of place in a regiment not described as 'light'.

(37) Officer, Luneburg Light Battalion. As in the K.G.L., the light infantry of the Hanoverian Army much resembled the British rifle regiments. However, the 'belgic' cap shown here would not be worn by a British unit, nor would blue trousers. Note the Running Horse badge and the yellow sash peculiar to Hanover.

(38) Sergeant, Grubenhagen Regiment. Another light infantry unit dressed after the British style. The sergeant's badge of rank appears to be the silver epaulettes.

be found in the 3rd Hanoverian Brigade under Colonel Hew Halkett. Here, too, the units were known by name and not by number, and considerable variety in uniform appears from battalion to battalion. Most, however, seem to have worn the British type of dress, ie, red for the line and dark green for the light; and the headdresses could be either a 'belgic' or light infantry cap. In other words, the same dress, practically, as the regular troops; and indeed, if any distinction did in fact exist, it was certainly not very evident.

DUTCH-BELGIAN CAVALRY

In 1815 the Dutch-Belgian cavalry, eight regiments strong, consisted of Carabiniers, Light Dragoons and Hussars, numbered consecutively, as in the British Army. Thus the 1st, 2nd and 3rd were Carabiniers, the 4th and 5th Light Dragoons, and the 6th and 8th Hussars. The 7th does not concern us here, because it was a colonial unit stationed in the East Indies. These units were formed mainly from individuals of the same nationality, so that the 1st and 3rd Carabiniers were Dutch and the 2nd Belgians, while in the light cavalry the 4th Light Dragoons and 6th Hussars were Dutch, and the 5th Light Dragoons and 8th Hussars Belgians.

The uniforms were of new design, because after Napoleon's first abdication in 1814, the Netherlands were restored to Austria, who appointed the Prince of Orange as Governor-General. In the southern provinces, a Belgian Legion had

BELGIAN CARABINIERS
1815
TROOPER

Painting by the author shows detail of the dress of the Belgian Carabiniers, the crested helmet distinguishing the 2nd Regiment. The coat is dark blue, the turnbacks, facings, and piping in red. Helmet is white metal with brass decorations. Cuff detail (red with red piping on a blue slash) is shown inset, normally concealed by the glove. The valise and saddle-cloth are dark blue with white and silver lace trimming respectively

been formed on March 4 of that year and clothed in a uniform of Austrian pattern; but this was more in the nature of a stop-gap, since on August 20 regulations were promulgated for the raising of a truly national army under the auspices of the Sovereign Prince of the United States of the Netherlands.

Dress Regulations were approved on January 9, 1815, but by the month of June only a proportion of the troops had been issued with the new clothing. In fact, at Waterloo, many of them wore a transitional uniform, which probably accounts for many contradictions one encounters in even contemporary descriptions.

The Carabiniers wore a helmet of classical design, with a black fur crest and a

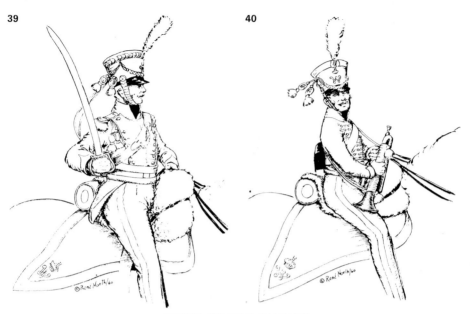

DUTCH-BELGIAN CAVALRY

(39) Officer, 5th Light Dragoons. Here again the pattern of dress recalls in some measure the British model. The sash, however, is orange—the colour of the Dutch reigning House.

(40) Trumpeter, 8th Hussars. This is a soldier wearing reversed colours, the normal dress for the regiment being a light blue jacket with red facings.

brass plate in the form of a lion's head (Fig 26) ; but there is evidence that this was worn by the 2nd Regiment only, the Netherlanders still retaining their former bicorne hat.

The first two regiments were dressed alike, except that the 2nd wore red epaulettes, while the 1st had blue shoulder-straps piped red. In the 3rd the uniform was as in the 1st, but the collar was yellow.

In the Light Dragoons, the differences were more pronounced. The 4th wore a blue jacket with red collar, cuffs and turnbacks, and a black bell-topped shako with a tall black plume, while the 5th were in green with yellow facings and a green shako. The 4th had white breeches and the 5th grey.

Both Hussar regiments were dressed in light blue throughout (but the 6th had a red collar) and black shakos with a white plume. Buttons were of white metal in all regiments, and the lacing of the Hussars was correspondingly white. However, some sources show red shakos, and other a blue collar and red pointed cuffs.

During the battle, the Carabiniers were in the 1st Corps under the Prince of Orange, as part of the Dutch-Belgian Heavy Cavalry Brigade. At midday they were in reserve near Mont St Jean, between the Nivelles and Genappe roads, and up to about half-past three they were engaged in defensive manoeuvring. They soon passed to the attack, however the 1st leading the charge, followed by the 2nd and 3rd.

The 4th Light Dragoons, at a strength of three squadrons, numbered about 700 all ranks under Lt-Col. Renno. It was part of the 2nd Light Cavalry Brigade,

TRUMPETER 1815

Belgian
Carabiniers

(now 3rd Lancers)

This trumpeter of the Belgian Carabiniers is from the same regiment as the trooper on page 37 and affords a good example of the 'reversed colours' worn by trumpeters in many regiments. The coat is red and the turnbacks, facings, and piping dark blue. The epaulettes were white lace and the helmet crest white instead of black, a further distinction peculiar to trumpeters in this particular regiment. The helmet is here worn with the chinscales down but the illustration on page 37 shows the appearance when worn 'up'.

one of the three which made up General Baron Collaert's Cavalry Division.

The 5th, under Lt-Col. de Merx, was in the 3rd Brigade under van Merlen. The total strength was 441 men in two squadrons; but they were held in reserve at Waterloo, having suffered heavily at Quatre Bras, mostly at the hands of the French Chasseurs à Cheval, whose uniform, curiously enough was very similar to their own.

The two regiments of Hussars were also in Collaert's Cavalry Division: the 6th in the 2nd Brigade and the 8th in the 1st. The latter regiment, having been raised as late as November 1814, comprised mostly young and inexperienced soldiers. Many were of French and German nationalities, as well as Belgian, which further increased the difficulties of Colonel Louis Duvivier, the commanding officer.

It was soon in action against the Horse Grenadiers of the Guard—a singularly unfortunate situation for such raw troops. To make matters worse, an order to left wheel, given in Dutch, was misunderstood, and the regiment turned about, to the joy of the French who pursued them hotly, inflicting heavy losses. Finally, reduced to the strength of a single squadron, it took part in Sir Hussey Vivian's and Vandeleur's cavalry movements in the closing stages of the battle.

DUTCH-BELGIAN ARTILLERY

In the Dutch-Belgian army the artillery consisted of nine batteries in all: 6 Dutch and 3 Belgian. Of these, the Belgians had one battery of horse artillery and two of foot (of which one—du Bois'—was in reserve), while the Dutch mustered two horse and four foot. All these units were equipped with

6-pounders except du Bois' which was a 12-pounder unit.

These troops wore the distinctive Netherlandish bell-topped shako, with a peak back and front, in close imitation of the Austrian headdress of the same period. The tall plume was black and the device in front took the form of crossed pieces in brass, surmounted by a crown in the same metal (Fig 28).

In the horse artillery the jacket was dark blue with a black collar and square cuffs of the same, bearing three-button slashes in the jacket colour. Shoulder-straps were blue, piped red, terminating in the characteristic Netherlandish padded wings of blue, with several lines of yellow piping. The garment was single-breasted and fastened by brass buttons; and the turnbacks were red, ornamented with blue grenades. The pockets at the back were simulated by a three-pointed line of piping with brass buttons in every angle. Grey overalls completed the outfit, with a red band bearing a row of brass buttons on the whole of its length.

The officers wore much the same, except that their collar and cuffs were made of velvet and the grenades on their turnbacks were gold, as were their epaulettes and overall-bands. The sash was orange, worn around the waist and knotted on the left hip.

Trumpeters appear to have worn either shakos or busbies. The former carried a white upright plume and the latter a red ball-tuft and bag, piped in yellow, with a tassel of the same colour. For the rest, the uniform was as above except for epaulettes with a blue strap, edged and fringed in yellow. The trumpet-cords, too, were yellow.

In the foot branch the dress was the same but for the absence of wings; and the drivers were distinguished by a red collar, shoulder-straps and cuffs, and white metal buttons. Some authorities, however, give a grey jacket instead of blue.

The Indian Brigade Artillery's uniform was somewhat different. The shako had no back peak and carried a red upright plume tipped black. The blue jacket was like the British garment in cut, with its square cuffs and lapels. Collar, shoulder-straps, cuffs and turnbacks were scarlet; and the square-ended loops appearing on the collar, lapels and cuffs were yellow, to correspond with the brass buttons. Trousers and gaiters are shown as white, but these may well have been a tropical issue, replaced by grey for home service.

DUTCH-BELGIAN INFANTRY

The infantry consisted of Dutch and Belgian units known respectively as North- and South-Netherlandish troops, differing in appearance mainly in the pattern of headdress, which for the latter was a 'belgic' shako (much resembling the British model), and a bell-topped variety, with peak back and front, for the former.

All battalions were dressed in single-breasted dark blue jackets and grey trousers, with collar, cuffs and piping in the facing colour, and nine brass buttons down the front. The turnbacks were red, while the cuff slashes were blue and the gaiters grey. The brass shako-plate, almost in the same design as the British, was stamped with the initial W in relief, and the plume and cords were white for the battalion companies and red for the flankers. The cockade for all troops was orange.

Flankers were further distinguished by large padded wings at the shoulders in the same cloth as the jacket, but bearing a number of white lines. The shoulder-straps—blue, with piping in the facing colour—were common to all companies.

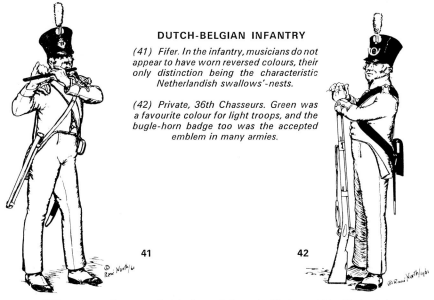

DUTCH-BELGIAN INFANTRY

(41) Fifer. In the infantry, musicians do not appear to have worn reversed colours, their only distinction being the characteristic Netherlandish swallows'-nests.

(42) Private, 36th Chasseurs. Green was a favourite colour for light troops, and the bugle-horn badge too was the accepted emblem in many armies.

41

42

Officers wore the same, but in finer cloth and with long skirts. Their shako-cords were of gold thread and they wore gold epaulettes, while their grey breeches were tucked into black Hessian boots. Gloves were white.

Drummers and fifers were dressed as the other ranks, but wore swallow-nests of a pattern peculiar to the Netherlands: a blue ground with two super-imposed chevrons of white lace—one upright and the other inverted forming a diamond shape in the centre. There was a horizontal white lace at the base of the swallow-nest, and in some cases a white fringe below this. In some Belgian units, however, the swallows-nests were white with a yellow lace and fringe.

The Dutch-Belgian battalions were distinguished by the following facing colours, worn on the collar, cuffs and piping:

1st and 9th, orange; 2nd and 10th, yellow; 3rd and 11th, white; 4th and 12th, red; 5th and 13th, crimson; 6th and 14th, light green; |7th and 15th, light blue, and 16th, pink.

The light infantry were termed Chasseurs or Jagers and wore green jackets similar in pattern to the Line, but with light yellow facings. The same bell-topped shako was in wear, but here it carried a green plume and a brass bugle-horn plate with the battalion numeral in the circle. The 16th, 18th and 27th were Dutch, while the 35th and 36th were Belgian.

Several units of Militia were also present at Waterloo, dressed much as the Regulars except that their white metal shako-plate was in the form of a semi-circle of rays spreading from a horizontal base, with the battalion numeral in the centre. The 5th Battalion appears to have worn a conical cap with this plate, and a white plume. The buttons were of white metal for all the Militia.

The 'Indian' infantry wore the bell-topped shako with a light blue-over-white plume (Fig 27). The blue jacket had a light blue collar and lapels, with brass buttons and yellow loops, including two on each side of the collar and three on each cuff, which were of British pattern. Piping on the shoulder-straps, lapels, cuffs and turnbacks was red, as well as on the three-point pockets, which carried a yellow loop at each button. Trousers and gaiters were white, but it is possible that they were exchanged for grey when on service in Europe.

BRUNSWICK CAVALRY AND ARTILLERY

The Brunswick Corps was part of the general reserve of the Netherlandish Army and consisted of one regiment of Hussars, one of Uhlans, two batteries of artillery and a body of infantry comprising three line battalions, three light battalions and one battalion of 'Avant-Garde' riflemen (Fig 21).

The whole of the Brunswick Army except the 'Avant-Garde' was dressed in the characteristic, essentially black uniform typical of that country. In fact, the British troops called them the 'Black Brunswickers'.

The Hussars, in black throughout except for light blue collars and cuffs, wore a white metal skull-and-crossbone device as a shako-plate (Fig 22). The origin of this badge is obscure: it has been used by the British 17th Lancers from very early days, and several German Hussar regiments wore it until 1918, while it also appeared in the Russian Army. In Great Britain it has been described as a memorial to the death of General Wolfe at Quebec, but a far more ancient origin seems likely. In the Brunswick Hussars the device was repeated on the black leather sabretaches of the rank-and-file, but for the officers it was replaced by the crowned cypher FW in gilt metal.

The Uhlans, in black likewise, wore the same light blue collar and cuffs as the Hussars (Fig 23). All this cavalry (ie, the 2nd Hussars, of four squadrons under Major Cramm, and the 2nd Squadron of the Uhlans) formed a brigade of some 900 men.

The Artillery, also in the traditional black uniform, wore yellow facings in both the horse and foot branches (Fig 24). In the Horse Artillery the shako carried the black plume of the cavalry, as well as the skull-and-crossbones plate in white metal, but in the Foot these devices were discarded in favour of a yellow pear-shaped pompon and a white metal grenade.

BRUNSWICK AND NASSAU INFANTRY

The three battalions of Brunswick Infantry of the Line were distinguished respectively by red facings for the 1st (Fig 25), green for the 2nd and white for the 3rd. The shako-plates, of white metal, were semi-circular in shape and stamped with the device of the White Horse of Brunswick and the motto *Nunquam Retrorsum*. This was surmounted by a small circle of the same metal bearing the battalion numeral, and the whole badge was worn high on the shako, partly covering the cockade.

The light infantry wore the same uniform but the shako here carried a white metal bugle-horn and a yellow-over-light blue pear-shaped pompon. The facing colours were: 1st Battalion, light blue (later pink-over-light orange), 2nd Battalion, yellow; and 3rd Battalion, orange.

Drummers of the Line units wore the same uniform as the other ranks plus swallows-nests at the shoulders. These were in the battalion facing colours (eg, red for the 1st Battalion) and did not carry a fringe at the lower edge.

The Brunswickers were first stationed in the rear of the centre of the Allied line, but were subsequently called to the extreme right, and by evening were in action opposite Hougoumont when the Duke gave the order for the general advance.

The army of the Duchy of Nassau consisted at Waterloo of eight battalions of infantry: a contingent of some 7,000 men in all (Fig 30). Five of these battalions were incorporated in the Netherlandish Army, and the remaining three formed an independent brigade under the orders of General Kruse. The five battalions in Dutch service were grouped into two regiments: the Regiment of Orange-Nassau (28th of the Line in the Netherlandish Army) and the 1st

Nassau Regiment.

The Regiment of Orange-Nassau and the 2nd Nassau Regiment were in Prince Bernard of Saxe-Weimar's 2nd Brigade of the 2nd Netherlandish Division under Lt-Gen. Perponcher: a part of the 1st Army Corps under the Prince of Orange.

Napoleon Bonaparte was born at Ajaccio on August 15, 1769, the son of a Corsican lawyer. The family was a large one and benefited greatly when Napoleon came to power; although his mother, immensely proud of her son, always suspected the 'rainy day'. His career in the French artillery, as well as his subsequent political and military successes are well known; but he remained the dedicated artillerist to the ?nd. At Waterloo, he commanded the French forces in the field. This print by Vernet dates from 1812 and was from a set commissioned by Napoleon.

43

Part 2:
The French Army

One battalion often decides the day
Napoleon I

FEW will dispute the contention that under Napoleon I the French army reached, if not the peak of its perfection, at least a state of grandeur which it has never since attained. There still exists in *l'épopée napoléonienne* a certain mystique—an irresistible combination of glamour, panache and colour—which no true Frenchman can forget, and no true francophile ignore; and although it is arguable that the ultimate result was good for France, it cannot be denied that the spirit lives on, even to-day. Madame Mère had every reason to be pleased with her son.

The army which he inherited from the Revolution may have lacked discipline by British standards, but it had the invaluable attribute of patriotism. Moreover, despite Bonaparte's manifest faults, it had faith in its leader, and in the Guard at any rate, continued to idolise *Le Tondu* until the end.

But the army that Napoleon put in the field after his return from Elba was no longer the formidable force of former years. That had been shattered in 1814 when it had been unequal to the task of preventing foreign troops from entering French territory. The French people were tired of wars and had lost faith in the Army; and indeed the Army, for all we know, may have lost faith in itself.

Hence the difficult problem of the Emperor in re-shaping that vast organization. Many of the old regiments were gone, and so was Berthier, the incomparable chief-of-staff. The new soldiers, many of them conscripts with little heart for the conflict, lacked the confidence of 1805 or the dash of a dozen years earlier. And yet, such was the effect of the Napoleonic presence that Waterloo became the 'damned near-run thing' of Wellington's famous phrase.

The blue coats of the French infantry were a legacy of the Revolution: the dress, in fact, of the National Guards who were thus distinguished from the white-coated Regulars. The regiments consisted, as before, of grenadier, battalion and light companies, the last two being called *fusiliers* and *voltigeurs* respectively.

By 1815 the old long-tailed coat had been discarded in favour of a short-skirted jacket, but the former turnback ornaments remained in wear: grenades for the grenadiers, a crowned letter N for the fusiliers and a bugle-horn for the voltigeurs. Trumpeters and drummers wore the green Imperial livery (Fig 50).

Badges of rank were those of the old Royal army—and indeed remained in wear until 1914: sergeant major, two gold or silver diagonal stripes above the cuff on both sleeves; sergeant, one similar stripe; corporal, two worsted stripes, as the sergeant major; lance corporal. one stripe. For the officers, rank was shown by the epaulettes, as follows: Colonel, two gold or silver epaulettes with bullion fringes; Major, the same but gold and silver; Battalion Commander, as Colonel, but no fringe on right epaulette; Captain, as Battalion Commander, but gold thread fringe; Lieutenant, the same, but red stripe along the straps; Sub-Lieutenant, the same, but two stripes. Regimental sergeant majors wore sub-lieutenants' epaulettes, but on opposite shoulders.

HORSE CHASSEURS OF THE GUARD

On January 13, 1800, a company of *Chasseurs à Cheval* of the Consular Guard was formed from a group of former *Guides de Bonaparte* on their return from Egypt. The unit subsequently reached regimental status, and when the Consular Guard became Imperial on May 18, 1804, the regiment altered its title accordingly. It eventually attained an establishment of eight squadrons, but was reduced to four at the First Restoration in 1814; and it was in those numbers that, Imperial once more, it fought at Waterloo, only to be disbanded in November 1815.

Detachments of this body were always on duty in close proximity to the Emperor, and its colourful dress is a prominent feature in many historical paintings, with its green plume tipped in red, and scarlet busby-bag. Indeed, Napoleon was much attached to his Chasseurs, and his familiar green coat was none other than the undress uniform of a colonel in the regiment.

The green jackets had red cuffs and *aurore* lacing, but the pelisse was red, with the same lacing. (Aurore is a colour peculiar to France: a salmon pink with a tinge of golden yellow.) Buttons were brass. The barrelled sash was dark green, with red barrels; and light buff breeches were worn with Hessian boots trimmed in *aurore*. A curved sword in a brass scabbard completed the outfit (Fig 31).

Moustaches were worn by all ranks, as well as the clubbed hair and gold earrings traditional to the Guard.

The horse-furniture consisted of a dark green schabraque and round valise, both trimmed in broad *aurore* lace and edged in narrow red piping. A large crowned eagle, also in *aurore*, was set at 45° in the rear corners.

On campaign, of course, the busby was quite plain and the pelisse was often discarded altogether. Breeches were replaced by grey overalls with a double

Models depicting two officers of the Horse Grenadiers of the Guard in their distinctive bearskin caps. Note the almost square-ended saddle - cloth, the holster-caps, and the valise with cloaks strapped on top of the latter. See next page for fuller description. (Courtesy Historex).

45

red band. Officers wore much the same, with gold lace instead of *aurore* and white fur on the pelisse, while the barrels of the sash were gilt (Fig 32).

HORSE GRENADIERS OF THE GUARD

This unit was simply the former Consular Guard regiment under a different name, consisting of four squadrons of two companies. Two more squadrons, both of Young Guard, were added in early 1813; and after becoming the *Corps Royal des Cuirassiers de France* at the First Restoration, the regiment resumed its old title during the Hundred Days.

The Horse Grenadiers were dressed much as their brethren of the Foot branch: bearskin cap and dark blue coat with collar of the same, white lapels and red cuffs with a white three-button slash (Fig 33). The turnbacks were red with *aurore* grenades, and the buttons were brass. Fringeless epaulettes of *aurore* were worn on both shoulders, with an aiguillette of the same colour on the right.

The bearskin, unlike in the Foot, had no plate, but carried the tall red grenadier plume. The top of the cap was covered in a circular piece of scarlet cloth, with two strips of *aurore* forming a right-angle cross. The chin-scales were brass and, as in the Foot, the hair was clubbed and powdered. Gold earrings, also, were worn, although strangely enough, no moustaches.

Breeches and gloves were light buff, the latter fitted with white gauntlet cuffs; and heavy cavalry boots completed the dress.

The saddle-cloth—almost square-ended—with its holster-caps and rectangular valise were all dark blue with *aurore* bands, which were double for the saddle-cloth and holster-caps and single for the valise. The white cloak, folded to show the red lining uppermost, was strapped above the valise.

Rousselot shows a Grenadier in the 1815 campaign dress, without the plume, and wearing a single-breasted short-tailed jacket (Fig 34). The breeches are grey, but otherwise the uniform is the same as full dress.

The sword, slightly curved, was carried in a brass scabbard. It had a brass hilt and a white knot.

DRAGOONS OF THE GUARD

Popularly known as the Empress's Dragoons, this regiment was raised in July 1806 at a strength of three squadrons, but by the time of Waterloo it had been increased to five. For a short time it served the King as the *Corps Royal des Dragons de France* in 1814, reverting to its old title on April 8, 1815; but after Waterloo, the survivors, withdrawn south of the Loire, were disbanded in the latter months of the year.

The Guard Dragoons differed from the Line chiefly in the helmet, which carried a leopard-skin turban covering the peak (Fig 35). Also, as a Guard unit, their collars were in the coat colour and the cuffs and their slashes were red and white respectively, while the white lapels further emphasized the Guard status. The coat was dark green, with *aurore* fringeless epaulettes and aiguillettes of the same colour. All buttons were brass.

The helmet was brass throughout and carried a scarlet plume in full dress. The waistcoat was white, while the gloves and breeches were light buff.

For horse-furniture, the Dragoons had a dark square-ended saddle-cloth, edged in two bands of *aurore*, and displaying an Imperial crown in the same colour in the rear corners. The rectangular valise and two-tier holster-caps were green likewise, with the same two bands to agree with the saddle-cloth. The white and red cloak was strapped to the valise as in the Horse Grenadiers.

On active service the uniform was the same except for the plume, aiguillettes, and the buff breeches which were then replaced by grey.

LANCERS OF THE GUARD

The lancer formation of the Guard consisted mostly of the 2nd Regiment, since the original Polish Lancers had been reduced to the single squadron which accompanied the Emperor to Elba. The latter, however, was incorporated in this regiment, and took precedence over the other four.

The 2nd Regiment was formed almost entirely from the 1st Hussars of the Kingdom of Holland, being completed to four squadrons with details from the Dutch Gardes du Corps and 3rd Hussars. In 1812 a fifth squadron was raised from French nationals and from a squadron of Hussars of the ex-Dutch Guard recently returned from Spain.

It was almost by accident that this regiment became Lancers, for they were originally destined to be Cuirassiers. Napoleon, in one of his rare oversights, had not noticed the tall stature of the men and had ordered light mounts. Clearly, 6-foot men, heavily armed, and riding 14-hand horses, would have been ludicrous.

The uniform, worn for the first time or August 15, 1811, was all red (Fig 36). The lance-cap carried a tall white plume, yellow cap-lines and a brass plate. The facing colour of dark blue was worn on the collar, lapels, turnbacks, piping, cuffs and double overall-bands; and all buttons were brass. A yellow epaulette with a blue crescent protected the right shoulder, while the left carried a yellow shoulder-cord retaining an aiguillette of the same colour.

The dark blue shabraque was edged in two yellow bands, and a large yellow crowned eagle was set at 45° in the rear corners. The black sheepskin had yellow dog's-teeth, and the round valise was red, with yellow borders at the ends.

The Lancers were armed with the same light cavalry sword as the Chasseurs, and the lance carried a white-over-red pennon.

On active service the lance-cap was covered in black oilskin, while the overalls were replaced by canvas trousers buttoned at the sides.

HORSE ARTILLERY OF THE GUARD

The 'birth certificate'—to quote Rousselot—of the Horse Artillery of the Guard was the Act of November 28, 1799, establishing a company of light artillery for the Consular Guard which, at the proclamation of the Empire, was raised to regimental status at a strength of three squadrons of two companies each.

It served in all the subsequent wars, and after the Campaign of France in 1814 the regiment was disbanded in July of that year. But on the Emperor's return from Elba in 1815 it was re-formed at an establishment of four companies serving six guns each.

For some unknown reason, most countries like to dress their horse artillery as Hussars, and France was no exception. In this case the uniform was dark blue throughout, including the pelisse, with red lacing and pointed cuffs of the same, while the busby had a red plume on the left, and a red bag and cords. However, it appears that in September 1813 the pelisses were unserviceable before even they were issued, since they had remained in store for three or four years and were hopelessly moth-eaten. True, the regiment drew new clothing before the start of the Waterloo campaign, but not in the Hussar pattern (apart from the black busby) for an inventory taken at its disbandment specifically mentions *coats*, as opposed to dolmans, as the jackets would have been called.

The hair was clubbed, in the Guard tradition, and there is also evidence of earrings; while moustaches were worn by all ranks except officers.

All horses were black, and the blue shabraques, terminating in long points, had a 3-inch edging and a crowned Imperial eagle in the points, all in red. The valise was round, in the same colour and edging.

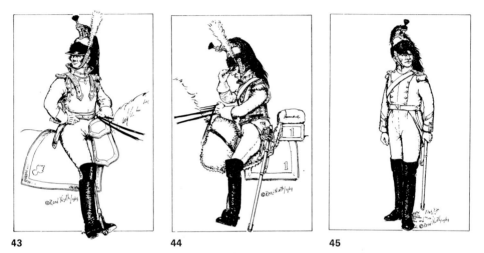

43   44   45

CUIRASSIERS

(43) Officer. Officers' horse furniture was dark blue and did not include a sheepskin. It was edged in silver lace, with a narrow red border on the outside. Contrary to the troopers, Cuirassier officers were clean-shaven.

(44) Trooper. The cuirassier sword was a straight thrusting weapon, which however had little effect on the British squares, since it was difficult for the heavy cavalry to reach their objective, hampered as they were by the rise in the terrain and the slippery nature of the soil, as much as by the deadly fire of the British.

(45) Sergeant. On dismounted duties the cuirass was laid aside, thus revealing lapels in the facing colour. Normally, black gaiters should be worn when dismounted, but it is possible that sergeants in charge of detachments may have retained their boots.

CUIRASSIERS

The Cuirassiers were the heavy cavalry of the French Army, descended from the regiments of horse raised as early as the 17th century. They were numbered consecutively from 1 to 14, but the last two regiments were newly-formed and were not present at Waterloo. However, the designation was not approved officially until September 24, 1803, although several cavalry regiments had already adopted the cuirass.

The various units were distinguished by the facing colours which were allotted in groups of three regiments as follows: Nos 1, 2 and 3, scarlet; Nos 4, 5 and 6, *aurore*; Nos 7, 8 and 9, primrose; and Nos 10, 11 and 12, pink. These colours appeared on the turnbacks and piping, as well as in the following arrangements: Nos 1, 4, 7 and 10, on collar and cuffs; Nos 2, 5 and 8 and 11, on cuffs only; Nos 3, 6, 9 and 12, on collar only.

The jackets were dark blue and worn under a steel cuirass with brass fittings and a scarlet lining which protruded at the openings. All blue parts were piped in the facing colours, and vice-versa; and blue grenades appeared on the turnbacks. The buttons were white metal and the epaulettes scarlet, except for the officers, where they were silver.

The helmet consisted of a steel skull with brass fittings. It had a fur turban, horsehair streamer at the back and a small tuft at the tip of the comb—all black; while the tall plume for dress occasions was scarlet. The front peak was made of black leather, sometimes bound in brass.

Breeches were light buff for full dress, and grey (buttoned at the sides) for service wear. Heavy boots were worn for mounted duties and black gaiters for dismounted.

Horse-furniture consisted of a dark blue saddle-cloth with square corners, edged in broad white lace, and a rectangular valise in the same pattern. The regimental numeral, or a grenade, appeared in the rear corners and in the centre of the valise-ends; and the white cloak (folded to show the scarlet lining uppermost) was strapped above the valise. Finally, a white sheepskin, edged in dog's-teeth of the facing colour, covered the saddle.

DRAGOONS

At the beginning of Napoleon's reign there were some 30 dragoon regiments, distinguished by facing colours of scarlet, crimson, pink, primrose and *aurore* for every group of six regiments. Thus, the regiments present at Waterloo would be dressed in a green coat with facings as follows:

Regiment	Lapels and turnbacks	Collar	Cuffs	Cuff-slashes	Pockets
2nd	scarlet	green	scarlet	green	across
4th	scarlet	scarlet	scarlet	scarlet	across
5th	scarlet	green	scarlet	green	vertical
6th	scarlet	scarlet	green	scarlet	vertical
7th	crimson	crimson	crimson	crimson	across
12th	crimson	crimson	green	crimson	vertical
13th	pink	pink	pink	pink	across
14th	pink	green	pink	green	across
15th	pink	pink	green	pink	across
16th	pink	pink	green	pink	vertical
17th	pink	green	pink	green	vertical
20th	primrose	green	primrose	green	across

The helmet was brass throughout, with a brown fur turban, while gloves and breeches were light buff. On active service, however, the helmets were often encased in a cloth cover; and grey or drab overalls were worn, buttoned over the breeches, reaching down to the ankles.

Dragoons are really mounted infantry and, therefore, they included such features as élite companies, pioneers and side drummers. The élite companies and pioneers wore bearskin caps with a scarlet plume; and the infantry connection was further emphasized by the black gaiters worn on dismounted duties.

Horse-furniture consisted of a white sheepskin with a dog's-teeth lining in the facing colour, while the saddle-cloth and valise were green, with border and numeral in white.

Officers' uniform was basically identical except for the silver epaulettes.

White metal buttons were worn by all ranks.

The Dragoons were armed with straight brass-hilted swords carried in a black scabbard with brass fittings, as well as a brace of pistols and a short musket with its bayonet.

A colonel of the 1st Regiment of Dragoons (which was not actually present at Waterloo) in full dress—known as 'grande tenue'—portraying the typical appearance of a field officer. Compare detail with drawing 48 opposite. This is a Vernet print published in 1812, part of the series specially commissioned by Napoleon.

DRAGOONS

(46) Pioneer. Pioneers' uniform conformed closely to the infantry pattern for that rank, ie, a bearskin cap, white gauntlets and a white leather apron, in this case turned up on the left hip for easier riding. The traditional beard of the sapper was also worn and the axe was carried in a white leather bandolier slung over the left shoulder. In the French Army, pioneers were distinguished by crossed axes above the elbow on both sleeves; otherwise the uniform was the same as for other ranks except for the bearskin which had scarlet ornaments. The cross on the top of the cap was white on a scarlet ground.

(47) Officer, Elite Company. The elite company was the grenadier company of the Dragoons, and thereby entitled to the bearskin cap. For the officers, the rest of the uniform was identical with their colleagues in the other companies, but for other ranks it included scarlet epaulettes.

46

47

(48) Field Officer. These were distinguished by bullion-fringed epaulettes and a double row of silver lace on the horse-furniture. Commanding officers of regiments wore a white plume.

(49) Dragoon. Contrary to the Dragoons of the Guard, those of the Line had black leather peaks on their helmets. The cloak, as in most of the French cavalry, was white with a scarlet lining. When not in wear it was folded and strapped to the valise with the lining uppermost.

48

49

Another Vernet print showing a major of the chevaulégers-lanciers in full dress. A full description of this dress is given below. The officers, needless to say, did not carry lances. Note the smaller stature of the horse. This print dates from 1812.

LANCERS

When Napoleon considered the devastating effect which enemy lances had on his cavalry's morale he decided to equip some of his forces with that weapon, bearing in mind, too, its effectiveness on retreating troops. Thus, on June 18, 1811, he published a decree authorizing the establishment of nine regiments of *chevaulégers-lanciers*, mostly by converting several dragoon regiments to the new light-horse branch. The last three regiments, however, were Polish and dressed as such.

The dark green colour of the dragoon coat was retained, as well as the brass helmet, but the horsehair streamer was now replaced by a black fur crest (white or scarlet for trumpeters) over the comb. A scarlet plume was worn in full dress, except in the élite company of the 6th which had a scarlet crest and a white plume.

The breeches were green for all ranks, with a 1-inch yellow lace down the outer seam and forming an Austrian knot or a bastion on the thighs, while a similar lace and tassel appeared on the Hessian boots.

Facing colours for the six regiments present at Waterloo (worn on collar, lapels, cuffs, turnbacks and piping) were as follows: 1st Regiment, scarlet; 2nd, *aurore*; 3rd, pink; 4th, crimson; 5th, light blue (Fig 40); and 6th, red. The piping appeared on the back pockets of the jacket and around the shoulder-straps; but the élite companies wore scaret epaulettes.

Apart from the lance, with its red-over-white pennon, commemorating in Polish national colours the origins of this arm, the lancer was armed with a brass-hilted light cavalry sword in a steel scabbard; and his horse, of between 14 and 15 hands, carried a white sheepskin lined in the facing colour, with a round valise in green, edged yellow.

At Waterloo, the 3rd and 4th Lancers were the first to counter-attack the Household and Union Brigades after their famous charge toward La Belle Alliance. They pursued the red-coats back to the British lines, but were themselves beaten back by the 12th and 16th Light Dragoons.

CARABINIERS

(50) Kettle-Drummer. In the French Army, kettle-drums were a little smaller than the British variety; and the banners were shaped in panels, in a manner common to many Continental countries. In the Carabiniers, this was sky-blue in colour, with white embroidery, and the drummer wore reversed colours, ie, a sky-blue jacket with white collar and lace. The epaulettes, chevrons and turnbacks were white, and the helmet-crest and saddle-cloth were sky-blue, the latter with white ornaments.

(51) Field Officer. The Carabinier cuirass, like that of the Cuirassiers, fitted over a detachable lining which protruded at the openings, but in this case it was dark blue, edged in white. The helmet-plate and chin-scales (with side-bosses carrying a gilt star) were of white metal for all ranks. Note also the great width of the scales at the top and the straight base of the bosses.

50   51

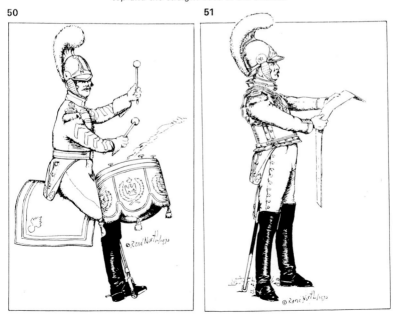

52   53

CARABINIERS

(52) Sergeant. As in the Cuirassiers, the cuirass was discarded for dismounted duties. The cross-belts—rather unusual in a cavalry regiment—were buff edged white; and the sergeant's stripes were silver piped in dark blue.

(53) Trooper. Horse-furniture was sky-blue (including the dog's-teeth) with white ornaments, and the cloak was folded to show the sky-blue lining uppermost. The round valise is somewhat unusual for a heavy cavalry unit.

CARABINIERS

The two Carabinier regiments, originally dressed in blue with black bearskin caps, suffered such heavy losses in 1809 that the Emperor decided to provide them—much against their will, incidentally—with a new uniform comprising a helmet and cuirass. He would have preferred a red coat for these troops, but finally agreed to white, probably for reasons of economy. The sky-blue facing colour, worn on collar, piping, cuffs and turnbacks, combined with the scarlet crest and épaulettes to produce a most colourful effect, contrasting very happily with the black coats of the horses.

A curious feature of this very resplendent body was that, whereas the rank-and-file wore brass helmets and cuirasses, the officers' pattern was made of copper; and the drab overalls, worn on active service, were distinctly khaki in colour, with buttons of the same.

Trumpeters, originally in reverse colours, wore the green Imperial livery after 1812. The white helmet-crest remained in wear and they continued to ride grey horses.

The only distinction between the two regiments lay in the cuff-slashes: white with sky-blue piping for the 1st, and sky-blue with white piping for the 2nd.

Although nominally in the Guard, at Waterloo the two regiments formed the 1st Brigade of the 12th Cavalry Division under Baron Blanchard.

HUSSARS

Unlike their British counterparts, the French Hussars were not converted from Light Dragoons—or in this case Chasseurs—but were the descendants of regiments raised specifically as such and based on the Hungarian pattern. Indeed, their very name derives from the Hungarian word *huszár*, meaning 'twentieth' and denoting the one man in twenty selected by ballot for military service.

Their dress, modelled on the Hungarian national costume, lent itself admirably to colourful interpretation, and Napoleon's Hussars were particularly resplendent, especially since every unit had its own uniform. The regiments at Waterloo should have been dressed as shown in Figs 41 to 45 according to the following tables, but it is likely that much improvisation took place. Horse-furniture was similar to the Chasseurs'.

Regiment		Jacket	Collar	Cuffs	Lacing
1st	(Fig 41)	light blue	light blue	scarlet	white
4th	(Fig 42)	dark blue	dark blue	scarlet	yellow
5th	(Fig 43)	mid-blue	mid-blue	mid-blue	primrose
6th	(Fig 44)	scarlet	dark blue	dark blue	yellow
7th	(Fig 45)	green	scarlet	scarlet	primrose

Regiment	Pelisse	Overalls and Stripes	Valise and Numeral	Dog's Teeth
1st	light blue	light blue/scarlet	light blue/white	scarlet
4th	scarlet	dark blue	dark blue/yellow	scarlet
5th	white	light blue	light blue/primrose	light blue
6th	dark blue	dark blue/scarlet	dark blue/yellow	scarlet
7th	green	green/scarlet	green/primrose	scarlet

The buttons were either brass or silver according to the lacing.

CHASSEURS A CHEVAL

This arm of light cavalry corresponded with the light dragoons of the British Army, and numbered as many as 24 regiments in the early days of the Empire, subsequently reaching a total of 29. By 1815, however, the number had been considerably reduced, and at Waterloo no more than seven regiments were present.

The uniform was dark green throughout and the head-dress was the regulation shako with white-metal fittings to conform with the buttons. The full-dress plume, rising from a ball-tuft in the company colour, was usually green topped red, or the reverse.

Many types of coat were worn, ranging from the hussar-type jacket to the long-tailed coat and finally the short jacket of 1812, with or without lapels and comprising turnbacks in the facing colour, carrying a green bugle-horn. The breeches were trimmed with white lace down the seams and forming bastion loops on the thighs, but the overalls, green likewise and fitted with leather grips inside the leg, could have the same white lace or a double band in the facing colour.

The latter was allotted on a three-regiment basis, so that the regiments at Waterloo would have appeared thus: 1st, scarlet collar and cuffs (Fig 39); 3rd, scarlet collar and green cuffs; 4th, primrose collar and cuffs; 6th, primrose collar and green cuffs (Fig 38); 8th, green collar and pink cuffs; 9th, pink collar and green cuffs; 11th, crimson collar and green cuffs.

All green parts were piped in the facing colour, and vice-versa.

The horse-furniture was simply a white sheepskin with dog's-teeth in the facing colour, and a round valise in green bearing a white numeral within a circle of the same.

The Chasseurs carried a curved brass-hilted sword in a plain steel or black scabbard with brass fittings. The bayonet was worn in a brown leather scabbard suspended from the white waistbelt, beside the sword.

54   55   56   57

GRENADIERS OF THE GUARD

(54) Drum Major. French drum-majors were resplendent figures, particularly in the Guard, covered as they were in a profusion of gold lace. The upright plume was white and the feathers pink, blue and white. Coat and collar were dark blue and the remainder white. The staff was of natural wood with gilt fittings and gold cords.

(55) Pioneer. The pioneers had no plate on their bearskins, which carried mixed red-and-yellow cords. These colours appeared also in the epaulettes and lace, but the crossed axes, on both sleeves, were yellow edged in red. All leather-work, including the apron and gauntlets, was white, and the metal-work brass.

(56) Officer. Officers were dressed much as the other ranks, except for a gilt cap-plate and gold epaulettes. Note the short grenadier officer's sword.

(57) Grenadier. The scarlet plume and cords were discarded on active service, but the tricolour cockade remained. White waistcoats appear to have been worn in service dress, as well as the blue.

GRENADIERS OF THE GUARD

The Grenadiers of the Guard originated on November 28, 1799, as the *Garde des Consuls,* and became 'Imperial' when Napoleon assumed the crown in 1804. The uniform has suffered much misrepresentation over the years, but the main attributes of the Guard units, it will be recalled, were the collar in the same colour as the coat, and red cuffs with white slashes : all of which were present in the Grenadiers.

The bearskin cap, with its circular red patch at the back bearing a white grenade, had a copper plate showing the Imperial eagle in embossed relief. (The earlier brass version survived in gilt for the officers, drummers and the like.)

The dark blue coat with its white lapels and scarlet epaulettes needs no description, but the white breeches and gaiters were replaced on campaign by dark blue trousers and black gaiters, and there can be little doubt that this was the dress worn at Waterloo.

NCOs and all privates carried the short *sabre-briquet* with a white sword-knot terminating in a scarlet tassel, but for sergeants this was mixed red and gold, to correspond with the same colours in their epaulettes. The black pouch-flap bore copper ornaments in the form of a crowned eagle flanked by four grenades set at 45° in the corners.

During the Hundred Days the four regiments of Grenadiers, totalling 4,140 men, formed the 1st Brigade of the Guards Division under Friant.

FOOT CHASSEURS OF THE GUARD

It will be appreciated that the Imperial Guard, constituting virtually a small army in its own right, comprised representative regiments of most units in the parent body: hence the presence of light infantry regiments alongside the better-known Grenadiers, and differing from them mainly in the plume, epaulettes, cuffs and the absence of a plate on the bearskin.

This body was raised on January 3, 1800, as part of the Consular Guard at a strength of only 94 men, but was increased progressively until, by 1815, it had reached an establishment of four regiments totalling 4,600 men.

The plume, discarded on active service, was half green and half scarlet, the scarlet uppermost ; and the epaulettes had a green strap, with a scarlet crescent and fringe. The scarlet cuffs, as befitted light infantry, were pointed and piped in white, and as a further distinction, the turnbacks carried an *aurore* bugle-horn on the outer flaps, to correspond with a grenade of the same colour on the inner (Fig 50). The sword-knot was green, with a scarlet tassel-head.

The Chasseurs were on duty on June 17 as the Emperor's bodyguard, and one regiment camped in the orchard of the *Ferme du Caillou,* where Napoleon spent the night before the battle. They also played a leading part in the evening, on the battlefield of Waterloo, when their resolute stand almost tipped the balance in France's favour. Indeed, it was the commanding officer of the 1st Regiment, Count Cambronne who, when summoned to surrender, shouted the ribald expletive which went down in history as *le mot de Cambronne;* an attractive incident which, apocryphal or not, aptly sums up the undaunted spirit of those magnificent soldiers.

TIRAILLEURS AND VOLTIGEURS OF THE GUARD

These troops—two regiments of Tirailleurs and two of Voltigeurs—were part of the Young Guard and formed two brigades. The Young Guard was instituted as a reserve and training-ground for the Old Guard ; therefore its members did not wear the uniform to which they aspired later.

Their dress was, in fact, simply that of the infantry of the line, but with blue lapels instead of white and with the pointed cuff which denoted light infantry. In addition, the epaulettes proclaimed a *corps d'élite*, and indeed the Tirailleurs and Voltigeurs could, at first glance, be mistaken respectively for grenadiers and voltigeurs of a line regiment.

Both Tirailleurs and Voltigeurs were descended from a somewhat complex organization of units within the Guard. On October 28, 1808, a regiment of Conscripts of the Guard was founded, to be split, in the following year, into Conscript Chasseurs and Conscript Grenadiers. Meanwhile, on June 16, 1809, two further regiments were raised: one of Tirailleurs-Grenadiers and another Tirailleurs-Chasseurs; and on December 30, 1810, the Tirailleurs-Chasseurs and Conscript Chasseurs were amalgamated to become Voltigeurs (Fig 47) and the Tirailleurs-Grenadiers and Conscript-Grenadiers became Tirailleurs (Fig 46).

At Waterloo they were under the command of Count Duhesme, but do not appear to have contributed in any outstanding manner to the events of the day.

58   59

FOOT ARTILLERY OF THE GUARD

(58) Field Officer. This officer is wearing the chin-scales hooked up to the back of the bearskin: a position much favoured in preference to using the scales as a chin-strap. The gilt gorget denotes that the officer is on duty. Note also the black leather gauntlets.

(59) Gunner and Sergeant. Equipment is of infantry pattern: fawn calfskin pac surmounted by the rolled greatcoat, in this case dark blue. On Sunday parades at home sergeants wore white breeches and stockings, as well as white gloves, and shoes with brass buckles.

FOOT ARTILLERY OF THE GUARD

Raised on April 12, 1808, at a strength of six companies, this unit was clothed much as the Artillery of the Line, except for the scarlet epaulettes denoting a *corps d'élite*. By 1815 the earlier shako had been replaced by a bearskin cap with scarlet ornaments and a leather peak (the latter, presumably, to shield the eyes when laying over open sights); and as in most of the Guard units, powdered hair and gold earrings were worn.

The uniform was dark blue throughout except for scarlet cuffs, turnbacks and piping: a sombre outfit—especially when worn with black gaiters—which the brass buttons and white belts did little to alleviate. Yellow grenades appeared on the scarlet crowns of the caps and on the turnbacks, and the sword-knot was scarlet; while the black pouch carried a brass device in the form of the Imperial eagle over crossed pieces.

Officers' uniform was practically identical except for gold epaulettes and riding boots. They retained the scarlet plume (discarded on active service) and brass chin-scales of the other ranks, but their cords and flounders were gold.

The Foot Artillery of the Guard, at its zenith, had risen to as many as six companies in the Old Guard and 16 in the Young, plus a company of *ouvriers-pontonniers* to deal with bridge building; but at the start of the Hundred Days it could muster no more than six companies all told, plus the company of pontoon men. The companies were equipped with eight guns each, and the whole body was under the command of Baron H. Lallemand.

SAILORS OF THE GUARD

The original battalion of *Matelots de la Garde*, raised on September 17, 1803, was almost entirely destroyed in Spain in 1808. However, the corps was reorganized on March 27, 1809, as a 'ship's company' of five squads. On June 30, 1814, it was disbanded, but 21 sailors and an ensign accompanied the Emperor to Elba; and during the Hundred Days the strength was increased to 150 all ranks. Final disbandment took place on August 15, 1815.

The sailors were hardly nautical in their appearance, but, rather unaccountably, had much of the Hussar (Fig 48). True, the uniform was dark blue throughout, except for scarlet cuffs, but all lacing, including that on the shako, was *aurore*; and the latter bore a scarlet plume for full dress, while the buttons and fringeless epaulettes were brass. On active service, however, a short double-breasted jacket was worn, with blue cuffs, but devoid of 'Hussar' lacing; and the shako was covered in black oilskin (Fig 49).

The officers' bicorne hat, with or without plume, was worn 'fore-and-aft', and their coat was long-skirted, with blue lapels open in front to reveal a scarlet waistcoat laced Hussar fashion. The breeches had a number of bastion loops on the thighs, according to rank, which was also indicated by gold epaulettes on both shoulders and aiguillettes on the right. The cuffs were blue, and all lacing gold, including the edging and tassels of the Hessian boots.

Drummers and trumpeters wore the other ranks' uniform, but in light blue. The lacing was mixed *aurore* and scarlet (except on the shako-band) and they wore *aurore* trefoils instead of epaulettes. In service dress the jacket was like the other ranks, but in light blue.

During the battle of Waterloo this small company of 147 men was attached to the Old Guard, but information on its part in the battle is not readily available.

SAPPERS OF THE GUARD

Towards the end of 1810 a company of Sappers was raised, as part of the Imperial Guard, whose duty consisted mainly in providing the fire-fighting services in the Imperial palaces of Paris, St Cloud, Versailles, Meudon, Rambouillet, Compiègne, Fontainebleau and other residences as required. Thus, when the Guard was detailed for active service, three sections of the company, under a captain, manned the six horse-drawn fire-engines attached to Imperial Headquarters.

In early 1812 the infantry of the Guard was formed into four divisions, each embodying a company of Sappers; but of these four companies, the Sappers of the Guard were attached to the Old Guard (ie, Grenadiers and Chasseurs), while the other three were drawn from the Line and attached to the Young Guard formations. Presumably, therefore, the 125-man company present at Waterloo must have been stationed in the vicinity of the *Ferme du Caillou*, where the Emperor spent the night before the battle.

The uniform was that of the Artillery of the Guard, but with black collar, lapels and cuffs, while the headdress was the characteristic fireman's helmet of traditional design embellished with a black fur crest (Fig 37). It was made of steel, with brass fittings; and it is worthy of note that the Imperial eagle here was of a design peculiar to this unit: with the tips of the wings pointing upwards, and not downwards as in the conventional version.

Officers had the same uniform, but with gold epaulettes and heavy boots; and drummers wore a scarlet crest on their helmet. They also had a 1-inch gold lace around the collar, lapels and cuffs; and their epaulette fringes were mixed red and yellow. The drums were brass, with embossed grenades, and blue hoops bearing yellow grenades.

ARTILLERY OF THE LINE

By an interesting though unexplained convention, many countries choose to dress their gunners in more sober clothing than their other troops: usually with blue predominating, and nearly always with red facings. Thus the French artillery, from its earliest days, wore a dark blue coat with red cuffs, and the

60

FOOT ARTILLERY OF THE LINE

(60) Gunner. The scarlet epaulettes shown here are probably unofficial, but for the rest the uniform is regulation. The musket, of infantry pattern, was usually slung diagonally at the back, over the equipment, in order to leave the hands free. For a more detailed coverage of artillery uniforms and guns see 'French Napoleonic Artillery' by Michael Head, a companion volume to this.

OPPOSITE: By contrast this Martinet print of 1813 shows a cannonier in the long tail coat, and with more elaborate scarlet shako decoration and cords. The uniform is dark blue with scarlet piping and lining. Note the short 'sabre briquet'. The man is leaning against a 4 pdr. Gribeauval gun with port fire and sponge and rammer propped up inside the carriage.

A Paris chez Martinet, Libraire, rue du Coq H¹. 13. et 15.

CANONNIER.

en 1813.

uniform in wear during the First Empire differed but little from that of the *Ancien Régime:* dark blue throughout, with red cuffs, piping and turnbacks— the latter ornamented with blue grenades. Red lapels denoted craftsmen (*ouvriers*), and the buttons were brass for all ranks. Some authorities show red epaulettes, but these were probably unofficial, since these attributes were reserved for the Guard, Grenadiers and similar élite troops. The regulation jacket was simply the infantry pattern, with bastion-shaped shoulder-straps piped in red, and dark blue lapels and breeches replacing the white of the foot troops; while for headdress the standard black shako served the purpose, with brass fittings and red ornaments.

The horse branch, originally dressed as *Chasseurs à Cheval*, but in blue, modified their uniform progressively, until by the time of Waterloo they were wearing the Foot Artillery jacket, but with red epaulettes and pointed cuffs of the same colour (Fig 29). The dark blue breeches carried a 1-inch stripe down the sides and a bastion of the same on the thighs. The boots were the plain black Hessian variety, while the shako was the infantry pattern with ball-tuft, upper and lower edges, and double V-shaped chevrons at the sides, all in red.

On campaign the shako was protected by an oilskin cover, and dark blue overalls, piped red, replaced the full-dress breeches.

INFANTRY OF THE LINE

In the early years of the Empire considerable discretion had been left to commanding officers in matters of detail regarding the clothing of their troops. But by 1811 the situation was getting somewhat out of hand, and a commission was therefore constituted to draw up firm regulations in that connection, resulting in a standard uniform for all units, without any clear distinction

61

62

63

64

INFANTRY OF THE LINE

(61) Pioneer. Every regiment had its detachment of pioneers, mostly tall men and invariably bearded. On ceremonial occasions they marched at the head of the regiment, under the command of a sergeant. When not carried in the hand, the axe was enclosed in a white leather case, shaft uppermost, and attached to the soldier's equipment. Pioneers had their own type of sword, sometimes straight, sometimes slightly curved, and normally fitted with a brass hilt terminating in a cock's- or eagle's-head pommel. The musket was carried slung at the shoulder.

(62) Grenadier. Cap-lines had by now been discarded and replaced by scarlet V-shaped chevrons on the sides of the shako; but the plume, of course, was not worn on active service. Grenadiers' sword-knots were scarlet.

(63) Private. Since the battalion companies had no sword, and hence no sword-belt, the bayonet was carried in a plain brown leather scabbard attached to the front of the pouch-belt. Note also that whereas flank companies wore moustaches, the others were clean-shaven.

(64) Light Company. Voltigeurs appear to have been allowed considerable latitude in the precise arrangement of the green and yellow colourings of their epaulettes. Thus, some regiments favoured green straps and yellow fringes, and others the reverse, while some even introduced red. The collar, however, remained universally yellow.

between regiments apart from the numeral on the shako-plate.

The shako remained as hitherto, but shed its cap-lines, while the dark blue coat, formerly open in front to show the waistcoat, now reached down to the waist, and the long skirts were considerably reduced in depth. Finally, the black gaiters were now cut short below the knees, after the British style.

The flank companies were distinguished as before by red epaulettes for the grenadiers and various combinations of yellow and green for the voltigeurs. In addition, grenadiers wore a broad red plume and red lace on the shako, while for voltigeurs these attributes were yellow. The battalion companies' shako was plain black (except tor the brass eagle plate and chin-scales, and the tricolour cockade) and instead of a plume it carried a 2-inch disc in the company colour: 1st, dark green; 2nd, light blue (Fig 53); 3rd, *aurore*; and 4th, violet.

On campaign, however, and especially in bad weather, a grey overcoat was worn, and the shako was covered in oilskin fitted with a flap which could be let down to cover the ears. Grenadiers and voltigeurs wore their epaulettes on the greatcoat (Fig 54); but the breeches and gaiters were then replaced by blue or white trousers, often tied round the ankles for greater comfort.

The equipment remained unaltered, ie, a calf-skin pack surmounted by the rolled greatcoat, and white cross-belts for the flank companies, carrying the short sword and bayonet on the left hip and the pouch on the right. The sword-knots were scarlet for the grenadiers and green for the voltigeurs. The battalion companies did not carry swords and therefore dispensed with the sword-belt, the bayonet being carried, in a manner peculiar to the French Army, in a brown leather scabbard attached to the pouch-belt, in front of the right hip (Figs 54 and 55).

65 **66** **67**

LIGHT INFANTRY

(65) Drummer. The uniform of drummers and musicians of light infantry tended to vary from regiment to regiment, probably according to the commanding officer's fancy. In some cases reversed colours were worn, while in others it was merely a case of adding lace (usually silver) to the regulation uniform. The shako, likewise, could be the regulation model or a coloured version which sometimes had little connection with regimental facings.

(66) Carabinier. The carabiniers were the grenadiers of the light infantry and in some units wore bearskin caps with scarlet fittings. Their pouch-flap was ornamented with a brass grenade, and the top of the gaiters was usually scarlet with tassels of the same colour.

(67) Private. Before 1812 many of the light infantry regiments wore the plume on the left of the shako, and bearing in mind the independent spirit of these units, it is quite likely that the custom may have lingered on. The cuffs were mostly of the square pattern shown here, but there were instances, also, of pointed cuffs being worn.

LIGHT INFANTRY

At the beginning of the Empire 26 light infantry regiments were in existence, but the number gradually increased until by 1814 they reached a total of 35. These were organized on the same basis as the line regiments: their equipment and drill were identical, and indeed they differed only in name and appearance.

Each regiment consisted normally of four battalions, but the number was often exceeded, especially when regiments were represented simultaneously in several theatres of war—on a pattern, in fact, which much resembled the British system.

The companies varied in number according to the period, ranging from 3 to 9 per battalion; and, as in the line, the first and last were flank companies, known here as Carabiniers and Voltigeurs respectively. The battalion companies were called Chasseurs.

The uniform was dark blue throughout, with black gaiters reaching to mid-calf. The piping was white and the buttons white metal. Carabiniers were distinguished by red shako fittings, collar and epaulettes, and Voltigeurs by yellow collars, and epaulettes in various combinations of yellow and green. Sometimes the Carabiniers retained the bearskin cap worn before the 1812 regulations became effective.

The Light Infantry was very active at Waterloo. At Hougoumont, for instance, it was Lieutenant Legros of the 1st Regiment, who, seizing an axe from a Pioneer in his battalion, broke down the gate. He rushed in at the head of his men, but was killed by the 2nd Foot Guards when they repulsed the attack. Likewise, the 13th, led by Marshal Ney in person, stormed La Haye Sainte with other units, and held the position for a considerable time.

THE 2nd SWISS REGIMENT

It is problematical whether the 2nd Swiss was in fact one of the four regiments that served Napoleon so brilliantly before the First Abdication. At the Return from Elba, the Swiss, true to their latest agreements, remained loyal to the King of France and were consequently discharged by the Emperor. However, some were persuaded to return to his service and a battalion of 730 men was raised by the brothers Stoffel under the title of *Deuxième Régiment Suisse.* It was then placed in Vandamme's III Corps as part of the 10th Infantry Division under Baron Habert, and brigaded with the 22nd and 70th Line Regiments.

The whole battalion was wiped out in the attack on the bridge at Wavre, and it is interesting to note that the widow of one of the NCOs, a certain Regula Engel who had followed her husband in all his campaigns, was wounded during the battle but lived on until 1853, when she died at Zurich aged 92 years.

The red uniform was traditional for the Swiss in French service (Fig 55) and remained in wear until they were finally disbanded in 1830.

Much has been said about 'Swiss mercenaries', but these troops were nothing of the sort; hence the reluctance of many of them to return to Napoleon after having sworn allegiance to the King of France as the legal sovereign of that country 'The Swiss', writes Captain de Vallière (*Honneur et Fidélité*) 'were fully-operational units which Switzerland lent to France. The Cantons had the right to recall their trops when necessary. This was a very special arrangement, supervised by the contracting states, and had nothing to do with the individual recruiting of mercenaries.'

Departments and Services

ENGINEERS

The *Génie*, or Corps of Engineers, already well established under the Monarchy, was re-organized on May 12, 1814, into three regiments of two battalions each. Every battalion consisted of six companies: five of sappers and one of miners. The 1st Regiment was stationed at Arras, the 2nd at Metz and the 3rd at Montpellier.

At the Second Restoration the three regiments were disbanded, but re-formed as a Royal corps one year later, at a strength of two battalions only.

The uniform was identical with that of the Sappers of the Guard except that the helmet was replaced by a regulation shako with a brass diamond-shaped plate and chin-scales, and that shoulder-straps were worn instead of epaulettes. Also, the jacket (open in front in the Guard) was here cut straight at the waist. Officers wore gold lace on their shako and the gold epaulettes of their rank, but otherwise their uniform was much the same as the men's except for dismounted-pattern boots with buff tops.

As in the other branches using large numbers of vehicles, the Engineers had their own corps of drivers: the *Train du Génie*. This body wore the traditional light blue-grey jacket of the French waggoners, but with the black collar, lapels and cuffs of the Engineers. The turnbacks were blue-grey and carried white grenades as ornaments.

The shako was the same as for the Sappers, that is all-black with a scarlet ball-tuft surmounted by a short plume of the same colour; but in this case the fittings were of white metal.

The breeches were buff and worn with heavy riding boots.

TRANSPORT

As in many other countries, the transport, or military train, was in the hands of civilian contractors: a somewhat unsatisfactory arrangement leading not only to considerable irregularities among the personnel, but also to frequent financial abuses. In France, one of these firms—the Breidt organization—proved so useless during the Polish campaign that Napoleon decided, in early March 1807, to raise a corps of military transport, capable of performing the same duties, but subject to military law. Thus, a decree signed on March 26 of that year provided for the establishment of eight battalions of waggoners.

Their numbers increased rapidly, until by 1812 a total of 22 battalions was in existence. The 18th, called the Ambulance Battalion, was raised as a pack-mule unit for service in Spain.

The first uniform was brown, with light blue-grey facings, worn with a civilian 'top hat' which was later replaced by a bicorme. This, however, was the costume worn by the civilian carters, for we find that in 1808 the Transport Corps was wearing a uniform in reversed colours, and that a shako had replaced the former hat (Fig 58).

It is interesting to note that the Artillery drivers formed two separate corps: one for the Guard and the other for the Line, both wearing the light blue-grey uniform peculiar to the transport branch. In the Guard they were distinguished by the scarlet ornaments on their shako, as well as by their scarlet epaulettes and piping (Fig 56), while in the Line the shako-ornaments were white

(Fig 57). The jackets, in the Guard as well as in the Line, are shown sometimes with dark blue lapels and sometimes with a single row of white-metal buttons: it is possible, therefore, that both patterns may have been worn simultaneously.

MEDICAL AND VETERINARY SERVICES

The medical service, as a regular corps in the French Army, dates back to the middle of the 18th Century, when the King authorized the surgeons attached to the Army of Westphalia to wear a uniform as a mark of authority, both on the battlefield and behind the lines. That was in 1757, and the dress was to consist of a grey coat with scarlet cuffs, waistcoat and breeches.

After the Revolution the uniform was changed to dark blue, with red facings for surgeons, green for apothecaries and black for physicians. Aprons, too, were issued, probably not without grim reason—and even here a nice order of seniority was observed, since the surgeons' aprons were to be white, the apothecaries' coloured and the medical orderlies' unbleached canvas. The physicians, probably because of their 'clean' work, had to do without.

The orderlies, unlike the British who were merely details from sundry regiments, were recruited as such since the Revolution and formed into companies on August 13, 1809. Their uniform consisted of a red-brown jacket with scarlet collar, lapels, cuffs and turnbacks, the latter bearing brown stars. The piping was white and the buttons white metal. The shako was regulation, with a white-metal diamond-shaped plate and scales, and a short scarlet plume; and the breeches were white, worn with black infantry-type gaiters.

Medical services at Waterloo were under the direction of Baron Larrey (Fig 59), a skilled and competent surgeon; and Percy's 'flying ambulances' were far in advance of their time.*

Nor was the veterinary side neglected. The corps, consisting presumably of officers only, was clothed in a dark blue coat with silver buttons and loops on the collar, the number of which denoted the rank. These officers were attached, in the main, to the cavalry regiments, and the type of unit was shown by the turnback-ornaments and the pattern of the boots. Thus, vets in the heavy cavalry (Cuirassiers, Carabiniers, Dragoons, etc) wore heavy boots and buff breeches (Fig 60), with silver grenades on the turnbacks, while those in the light branch (Hussars, Chasseurs, Lancers, etc) had blue breeches and Hessian boots, and silver bugle-horns as ornaments.

*See 'French Napoleonic Artillery' (Almark Publications) for scale drawings and details of these ambulances.

Appendix 1:
Order of Battle; Anglo-Allied Army, June 18th, 1815

Commander-in-Chief (Field-Marshal The Duke of Wellington)

I. Corps (The Prince of Orange)

1st Division (Maj-Gen. Cooke)
 1st Brigade (Maj-Gen. Maitland) 1st Foot Guards.
 2nd Brigade (Maj-Gen. Sir John Byng) 2nd Foot Guards, 2nd Bn. 3rd Foot Guards.
 British and K.G.L. field batteries.
3rd Division (Lt-Gen. Sir Charles Alten)
 5th Brigade (Maj-Gen. Sir Colin Halkett) 2/30th Foot, 33rd Foot, 2/69th Foot, 2/73rd Foot.
 2nd K.G.L. Brigade (Col. von Ompteda) 1st and 2nd Light Bns, 5th and 8th Line Bns.
 1st Hanoverian Brigade (Maj-Gen. Count Kielmansegge) 6 Hanoverian battalions.
 British and K.G.L. field batteries.
2nd Netherlandish Division (Lt-Gen. Baron de Perponcher)
 1st Brigade (Maj-Gen. de Bijlandt) 5 Netherlandish battalions.
 2nd Brigade (Prince Bernard of Saxe-Weimar) 5 Nassau battalions.
 1 Netherlandish horse battery.
3rd Netherlandish Division (Lt-Gen. Baron de Chassé)
 1st Brigade (Maj-Gen. Detmers) 6 Netherlandish battalions.
 2nd Brigade (Maj-Gen. d'Aubremé) 6 Netherlandish battalions.

II. Corps (Lt-Gen. Lord Hill)

2nd Division (Lt-Gen. Sir H. Clinton)
 3rd Brigade (Maj-Gen. Adam) 1/52nd Foot, 1/71st Foot, 2/95th Foot, 3/95th Foot.
 1st K.G.L. Brigade (Col. du Plat) 1st, 2nd, 3rd, 4th Line battalions.
 3rd Hanoverian Brigade (Col. Hew Halkett) 4 Landwehr battalions.
 British and K.G.L. field batteries.
4th Division (Lt-Gen. Sir Colin Colville)
 4th Brigade (Col. Mitchell) 3/14th Foot, 1/23rd Foot, 51st Foot.
 6th Brigade (Maj-Gen. Johnstone) 2/35th Foot, 1/54th Foot, 59th Foot, 1/91st Foot.
 6th Hanoverian Brigade (Maj-Gen. Sir James Lyon) 5 Hanoverian battalions.
 British and Hanoverian field batteries.

Corps of Prince Frederick of the Netherlands

1st Netherlandish Division (Lt-Gen. Stedman)
 d'Hauw's Brigade: 6 battalions.
 de Eerens' Brigade: 5 battalions.
 1 field battery of 8 guns.
Anthing's Netherlandish Indian Brigade: 5 battalions.
 1 field battery.

Cavalry

1st Brigade (Maj-Gen. Lord E. Somerset) 1st and 2nd Life Guards, The Royal Horse Guards, 1st The King's Dragoon Guards.
2nd Brigade (Maj-Gen. Sir W. Ponsonby) Royal Dragoons, Scots Greys, Inniskilling Dragoons.
3rd Brigade (Maj-Gen. Sir W. Dörnberg) 1st and 2nd Light Dragoons of the K.G.L., 23rd Light Dragoons.
4th Brigade (Maj-Gen. Sir J. Vandeleur) 11th, 12th, 16th Light Dragoons.
5th Brigade (Maj-Gen. Sir Colquhoun Grant) 7th and 15th Hussars, 2nd Hussars of the K.G.L.
6th Brigade (Maj-Gen. Sir Hussey Vivian) 10th and 18th Hussars, 1st Hussars of the K.G.L.
7th Brigade (Col. Arentschild) 13th Light Dragoons, 3rd Hussars of the K.G.L.
 1 howitzer battery, 5 horse batteries
1st Hanoverian Brigade   3 regiments.
Brunswick Cavalry   1 regiment + 1 squadron.
Netherlandish Cavalry   3 brigades (Trip, de Ghigny, van Merlen) (ie, 7 regiments + 2 half-batteries).

7th Division
7th Brigade, 2/25th Foot, 2/37th Foot, 2/78th Foot.
Hanoverian Reserve Corps, 12 Landwehr battalions in 4 brigade:

Reserve

5th Division (Lt-Gen. Sir Thomas Picton)
8th Brigade (Maj-Gen. Sir James Kempt) 1/28th Foot, 1/32nd Foot, 1/79th Foot, 1/95th Foot.
9th Brigade (Maj-Gen. Sir Denis Pack) 3/1st Foot, 1/42nd Foot, 2/44th Foot, 1/92nd Foot.
5th Hanoverian Brigade (Col. von Vincke) 4 Landwehr battalions.
British and Hanoverian field batteries.
6th Division
10th Brigade (Maj-Gen. Sir John Lambert) 1/4th Foot, 1/27th Foot, 1/40th Foot, 2/81st Foot.

4th Hanoverian Brigade (Col. Best) 4 Landwehr battalions.
2 British field batteries.
British Reserve Artillery: 2 horse batteries.
                           3 field batteries.
Brunswick Corps (The Duke of Brunswick)
2 infantry brigades of 3 battalions each.
Advance Guard; 4 companies of infantry; 1 detachment of cavalry.
2 batteries of artillery.
Nassau Contingent (Gen. von Kruse)
3 battalions.

Appendix 2:
Order of Battle; French Army, June 18th, 1815

Commander-in-Chief (Emperor Napoleon Bonaparte)

Imperial Guard (Lt-Gen. Count Drouot)

Old Guard, 1st, 2nd, 3rd Grenadiers.
    4th Grenadiers (1 battalion).
    1st, 2nd, 3rd, 4th Chasseurs.
1st Division Young Guard (Lt-Gen. Count Barrois).
    1st Brigade (Brig-Gen. Chartrand) 1st Tirailleurs, 1st Voltigeurs.
    2nd Brigade (Brig-Gen. Baron Guye) 2nd Tirailleurs, 2nd Voltigeurs
Light Cavalry, Old Guard (Lt-Gen. Count Lefebvre-Desnoëttes).
    Lancers (Lt-Gen. Baron de Colbert-Chabanis).
    Chasseurs à Cheval (Brig-Gen. Baron Lallemand).
Cavalry Reserve (Lt-Gen. Count Guyot).
    Grenadiers à Cheval (Brig-Gen. Jamin).
    Dragoons of the Guard (Lt-Gen. Baron Ornano).
Artillery (Lt-Gen. Baron Desvaux de St. Maurice).
    Horse Artillery (Col. Baron Duchand).
    Artillery Drivers (Col. Leroy).
    Foot Artillery (Gen. Baron Lallemand).
Transport, 1 squadron (Gubert).
Sailors of the Guard, 1 detachment (Tailade).
Gendarmerie d'Elite, 1 company (Col. Boissonnet).
Engineers, 1 detachment (Lt-Gen. Baron Haxo).

I. Corps (Lt-Gen. Drouet. d'Erlon)

1st Division (Lt-Gen. Allix de Vaux)
    1st Brigade (Brig-Gen. Quiot) 54th and 55th Line.
    2nd Brigade (Brig-Gen. Bourgeois) 28th and 105th Line.
2nd Division (Lt-Gen. Baron Donzelot)
    1st Brigade (Brig-Gen. Schmitz) 13th Light Regt, 17th Line Regt.
    2nd Brigade (Brig-Gen. Baron Aulard) 19th Line, 51st Line Regt.
3rd Division (Lt-Gen. Baron Marcognet)
    1st Brigade (Brig-Gen. Noguès) 21st Line, 46th Line.
    2nd Brigade (Brig-Gen. Grenier) 25th Line, 45th Line.
4th Division (Lt-Gen. Count Durutte)
    1st Brigade (Brig-Gen. Pegot) 8th Line, 29th Line.
    2nd Brigade (Brig-Gen. Brue) 58th Line, 95th Line.
1st Cavalry Division (Lt-Gen. Baron Jacquinot)
    1st Brigade (Brig-Gen. Brune) 7th Hussars, 3rd Chasseurs.
    2nd Brigade (Brig-Gen. Baron Gobrecht) 3rd Lancers, 4th Lancers
Horse and Foot Artillery and Engineers.

II. Corps (Lt-Gen. Count Reille)

5th Division (Lt-Gen. Baron Bachelu)
  1st Brigade (Brig-Gen. Baron Husson) 2nd Light Regt., 61st Line.
  2nd Brigade (Brig-Gen. Baron Campi) 72nd Line, 108th Line.
6th Division (Lt-Gen. Prince Jerome Napoléon)
  1st Brigade (Brig-Gen. Baron Baudouin) 1st Light Regt., 3rd Light Regt
  2nd Brigade (Brig-Gen. Soye) 1st Line, 2nd Line.
7th Division (Lt-Gen. Baron Girard)
  1st Brigade (Brig-Gen. Louis de Villiers) 11th Light Regt., 82nd Line
  2nd Brigade (Brig-Gen. Baron Piat) 12th Light Regt., 4th Line.
8th Division (Lt-Gen. Baron Foy)
  1st Brigade (Brig-Gen. Baron Gauthier) 92nd Line, 93rd Line.
  2nd Brigade (Brig-Gen. Jamin) 4th Light Regt, 100th Line.
2nd Cavalry Division (Lt-Gen. Count Piré)
  1st Brigade (Brig-Gen. Baron Hubert) 1st Chasseurs, 6th Chasseurs.
  2nd Brigade (Brig-Gen. Baron Wathiez) 5th Lancers, 6th Lancers.
Artillery and Engineers.

III. Corps (Lt-Gen. Count Vandamme)

8th Division (Lt-Gen. Baron Lefol)
  1st Brigade (Brig-Gen. Baron Billiard) 15th Light Regt, 23rd Line.
  2nd Brigade (Brig-Gen. Baron Corsin) 37th Line, 64th Line.
10th Division (Lt-Gen. Baron Habert)
  1st Brigade (Brig-Gen. Baron Gengoult) 34th Line, 88th Line.
  2nd Brigade (Brig-Gen. Baron Dupeyroux) 22nd Line, 70th Line, 2nd Swiss Regt
11th Division (Lt-Gen. Baron Berthezne)
  1st Brigade (Brig-Gen. Baron Dufour) 12th Line, 56th Line.
  2nd Brigade (Brig-Gen. Baron Legrade) 33rd Line, 86th Line.
3rd Cavalry Division (Lt-Gen. Baron Domon)
  1st Brigade (Brig-Gen. Baron Dommanget) 4th Chasseurs, 9th Chasseurs.
  2nd Brigade (Brig-Gen. Baron Vinot) 12th Chasseurs.
Horse and Foot Artillery and Engineers.

IV. Corps (Lt-Gen. Count Gérard)

12th Division (Lt-Gen. Baron Pecheux)
  1st Brigade (Brig-Gen. Baron Romme) 30th Line, 96th Line.
  2nd Brigade (Brig-Gen. Baron Schoeffer) 6th Light Regt., 63rd Line.
13th Division (Lt-Gen. Baron Vichery)
  1st Brigade (Brig-Gen. Baron le Capitaine) 59th Line, 76th Line.
  2nd Brigade (Brig-Gen. Count Desprez) 48th Line, 60th Line.
14th Division (Lt-Gen. Count de Bourmont)
  1st Brigade (Brig-Gen. Baron Hulot) 9th Light Regt., 111th Line.
  2nd Brigade (Brig-Gen. Baron Toussaint) 44th Line, 50th Line.
7th Cavalry Division (Lt-Gen. Baron Maurin)
  1st Brigade (Brig-Gen. Baron Vallin) 6th Hussars, 8th Chasseurs.
  2nd Brigade (Brig-Gen. Berruyer) 6th Dragoons, 16th Dragoons.
Horse and Foot Artillery and Engineers.

VI. Corps (Lt-Gen. Mouton, Count of Lobau)

19th Division (Lt-Gen. Baron Simmer)
  1st Brigade (Brig-Gen. Baron de Bellair) 5th Line, 11th Line.
  2nd Brigade (Brig-Gen. M. Jamin) 27th Line, 84th Line.
20th Division (Lt-Gen. Jeanin)
  1st Brigade (Brig-Gen. Bony) 5th Light Regt., 10th Line.
  2nd Brigade (Brig-Gen. Boudin) 47th Line, 107th Line.
21st Division (Lt-Gen. Baron Teste)
  1st Brigade (Brig-Gen. Baron Lafitte) 8th Light Regt., 40th Line.
  2nd Brigade (Brig-Gen. Baron Penne) 65th Line, 75th Line.
Foot Artillery and Engineers.

I. Cavalry Corps (Lt-Gen. Count Pajol)

4th Cavalry Division (Lt-Gen. Baron Soult)
  1st Brigade (Brig-Gen. Houssin de St. Laurent) 1st Hussars, 4th Hussars
  2nd Brigade (Brig-Gen. Baron Ameil) 5th Hussars.
5th Cavalry Division (Lt-Gen. Baron Subervie)
  1st Brigade (Brig-Gen. Count A. de Colbert) 1st Lancers, 2nd Lancers.
  2nd Brigade (Brig-Gen. Merlin de Douai) 11th Chasseurs.
Horse Artillery.

II. Cavalry Corps (Lt-Gen. Count Exelmans)

9th Cavalry Division (Lt-Gen. Baron Strolz)
  1st Brigade (Brig-Gen. Baron Burthe) 5th Dragoons, 13th Dragoons.
  2nd Brigade (Brig-Gen. Baron Vincent) 15th Dragoons, 20th Dragoons.
10th Cavalry Division (Lt-Gen. Baron Chastel)
  1st Brigade (Brig-Gen. Baron Bennemains) 4th Dragoons, 12th Dragoons.
  2nd Brigade (Brig-Gen. Berton) 14th Dragoons, 17th Dragoons.
Horse Artillery.

III. Cavalry Corps (Lt-Gen. Kellermann)

11th Cavalry Division (Lt-Gen. Baron L'Héritier)
    1st Brigade (Brig-Gen. Baron Picquet) 2nd Dragoons, 7th Dragoons.
    2nd Brigade (Brig-Gen. Baron Guiton) 8th Cuirassiers, 11th Cuirassiers.
12th Cavalry Division (Lt-Gen. Baron Roussel d'Hurbal)
    1st Brigade (Brig-Gen. Baron Blanchard) 1st Carabiniers, 2nd Carabiniers.
    2nd Brigade (Brig-Gen. Donop) 2nd Cuirassiers, 3rd Cuirassiers.
Horse Artillery

IV. Cavalry Corps (Lt-Gen. Count Milhaud)

13th Cavalry Division (Lt-Gen.Wathier, Count of St Alphonse)
    1st Brigade (Brig-Gen. Baron Dubois) 1st Cuirassiers, 4th Cuirassiers.
    2nd Brigade (Brig-Gen. Travers) 7th Cuirassiers, 12th Cuirassiers.
14th Cavalry Division (Lt-Gen. Baron Delort)
    1st Brigade (Brig-Gen. Baron Vial) 5th Cuirassiers, 10th Cuirassiers.
    2nd Brigade (Brig-Gen. Baron Farine) 6th Cuirassiers, 9th Cuirassiers.
Horse Artillery.

Appendix 3:
Glossary of Terms

Aiguillettes: Ornamental cords, usually gold, looped over one shoulder.
Austrian knot: Sometimes called 'Hungarian knot'. An ornamental pattern of cording, usually worn on the cuff, arranged in two large rings flanking a taller pointed shape in the centre.
Battalion companies: The main body of an infantry battalion (see 'flank companies').
Belgic cap: The British infantry shako introduced in 1811.
Bell-topped shako: A shako of inverted conical shape; ie, wider at the top than at the bottom.
Bicorne: A two-cornered hat.
Busby: A fur headdress worn by hussars and sometimes by horse artillery.
Busby-bag: A piece of coloured cloth, fitted to the top of the busby, and hanging to the side.
Cap-lines: The cords which connected the headdress with the body. Sometimes called 'body-lines'.
Chasseur: A French light infantryman or cavalryman.
Clubbed hair: A form of hair-dressing in which the queue did not reach below the nape of the neck.
Cockade: A rosette on the head-dress, often in national colours. In the British army it was black, and in the French (from the centre) blue, red and white.
Comb: The curved plate of upright metal surmounting a helmet.
Conical shako: The reverse of the bell-topped pattern; ie, smaller at the top than at the bottom.
Crest: A fur ornament, usually surmounting the comb on a helmet.
Cuff-slash: An upright strip of cloth, usually bearing three buttons, sewn over a straight cuff.
Dog's teeth: The zig-zag edging of the cloth lining under a sheepskin saddle.
Epaulette: A detachable shoulder-piece formed by a strap widening out in a crescent over the top of the shoulder and decorated with a fringe. Where the latter is absent, it is sometimes termed a 'counter-epaulette'.
Elite corps: Picked troops.
Facings: The parts of a uniform, such as collar, cuffs, etc, which are different in colour from the main garment.
Flank companies: The grenadier and light companies of an infantry battalion.
Hessian boots: Usually worn with hussar dress. The tops are cut in a heart-shaped pattern and often ornamented with lace and tassels.
Jacket: A short-tailed or tail-less garment, as opposed to a long-tailed coat.
Lace: Strips of ornamental braiding, mostly used as an edging to collars, cuffs, etc, and also for buttonhole loops.
Loops: See above.
Overalls: Long trousers with an under-boot strap or chain, worn by mounted troops.
Pack: A soldier's knapsack, carried on the back.
Pelisse: The hussar's fur-trimmed jacket, slung over the left shoulder when not in wear.
Piece: A gun-barrel.
Piping: The very narrow strips of coloured cloth, usually forming an edging to details of clothing, or marking the seams.
Primrose (colour): Light yellow.
Pompon: A ball-tuft on the headdress.
Sabretache: A pouch carried by cavalrymen, suspended by slings from the sword-belt.
Shabraque: A saddle-cloth with long rear points, often very ornate, usually used by light cavalry.
Shako: A rigid peaked headdress.
Shoulder-straps: Cloth shoulder-pieces originally intended to keep the shoulder-belts in position.
Streamer: The horsehair mane at the back of a heavy cavalry helmet.
Swallows'-nests: Small shoulder-ornaments, usually laced, denoting bandsmen.
Turban: The cloth or fur surrounding the base of a helmet.
Turnbacks: The parts of a coat-tail buttoned back ₂o reveal the lining.
Valise: A case, carried at the back of the saddle, containing a cavalryman's belongings.
Voltigeur: A French light infantryman.
Wings: Shoulder-ornaments in the form of a large crescent, usually denoting flank companies (in the British army).

Appendix 4 :
Select Bibliography

Major R. M. Barnes, *History and Regiments of the British Army.* Seeley Service, London.
A. H. Bowling, *British Infantry Regiments, 1660-1914.* Almark Publications, London, 1970.
W. Y. Carman, *British Military Uniforms.* Leonard Hill, London, 1957.
Paul Davies, *The Field of Waterloo.* Pan Books, London, 1970.
Major N. P. Dawnay and G. Haswell Miller, *Military Drawings . . . in the Royal Collection.* Phaidon, London, 1966.
Sir John Fortescue, *History of the British Army.* Vol. X.
Michael Head, *French Napoleonic Artillery.* Almark Publications, London, 1970.
Commandant H. Lachouque, *The Anatomy of Glory.* Brown University Press, Providence, Rhode Island, 1961.
C. C P. Lawson, *Uniforms of the British Army,* Vol. V. Kaye and Ward, London, 1967.
Paul Martin, *Military Costume.* Franckh, Stuttgart, 1963.
René North, *Military Uniforms, 1686-1913.* Hamlyn, London, 1970.
H. J. Ullrich and Paul Martin, *The Glamour of Uniform.* Franckh, Stuttgart, 1970.

(All the above books are widely available and are commended for further reading.)

Other military books published by ALMARK

BRITISH INFANTRY REGIMENTS, 1660-1914, by A. H. Bowling.

117 uniforms in colour, weapons, details, rare pictures and descriptive text.

GERMAN ARTILLERY, 1914-1918, by David Nash.

Guns, organisation, ranks, badges, colours, camouflage, and auxiliary equipment of the German gunners of the World War 1.

GERMAN COMBAT UNIFORMS, 1939-45, by S. R. Gordon-Douglas.

Concise guide to dress. badges and ranks, with many pictures and drawings, plus colour plates.

JAPANESE ARMY UNIFORMS AND EQUIPMENT, 1939-45, by Roy Dilley.

Profusely illustrated guide to Japanese uniforms, organisation, small arms, infantry weapons, ranks and badges, of World War 2 period.

SCOTTISH REGIMENTS, 1660-1914, by A. H. Bowling.

Histories of famous regiments, rare pictures, drawings and 115 uniforms shown in colour

INDIAN ARMY CAVALRY, by A. H. Bowling.

Uniforms and regiments of one of the most colourful fighting arms in history. Eight colour plates and many rare pictures.

FRENCH NAPOLEONIC ARTILLERY, by Michael Head.

Guns, equipment, organisation, transport, uniforms of one of the most interesting military periods, culminating in the Battle of Waterloo. Eight colour plates.

GERMAN INFANTRY, 1914-1918, by David Nash.

Weapons, uniforms, organisation, badges of the German infantry regiments of the First World War. Numerous pictures and colour plates.

BRITISH INFANTRY COLOURS, by Dino Lemonofides.

A concise guide to the Regimental Colours of the British Army, their evolution, design and history. Six superb colour plates.